SECTIONS

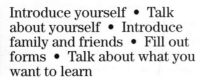

COMPLIMENTARY

MW01046147

Steven J. Molinsky
Bill Bliss

Deborah L. Schaffer
Carol H. Van Duzer
Carolyn Graham

PRENTICE HALL REGENTS
A VIACOM COMPANY

DEPARTMENTS

INTERVIEWS
Collecting and Reporting Information

DID YOU HEAR?
Listening Skills

LIFEWRITER
Writing Tasks

JOURNAL
Writing to Share Experiences, Ideas, and Creativity

DEAR NAVIGATOR
Your Letters about Culture and Customs

CULTURAL VIEWFINDER
Comparing and Contrasting Cultures

STAY IN SHAPE WORKOUTS
"Totally Physical" Action Sequences

CAREER PROFILES
Occupations

CONTRASTS
Problem-Posing Photo Essays

SYNTHESIZER
Cooperative Activities for Assessment and Teamwork

WordRaps™
Rhythm Poems

PUZZLER PAGE
Games, Crosswords, Word Scrambles

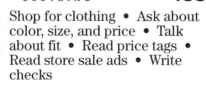

Navigator 1

Publisher   *Tina Carver*
Director of Production and
  Manufacturing   *Aliza Greenblatt*
Editorial Production/
  Design Manager   *Dominick Mosco*
Production Supervision
  and Composition   *Christine McLaughlin Mann*
Copyeditor   *Janet Johnston*
Production Assistant   *Jennifer Rella*
Pre-formatter   *Rose Ann Merrey*
Electronic Art Production   *Todd Ware, Marita Froimson*
                            Don Kilcoyne
Realia   *Ken Liao, Warren Fischbach, Don Kilcoyne*
         Dean Fiorino
Manufacturing Manager   *Ray Keating*
Cover Coordinator   *Merle Krumper*
Photo Researcher   *Rhoda Sydney*
Interior Design   *Todd Cooper, Bill Smith Studio*
Illustrator   *Richard Hill*
Photographer   *Paul Tañedo*
Associate Photographer   *Rhonda Rynex*
Photography Assistant   *Charles Chaleunrath*

© 1996 by PRENTICE HALL REGENTS
Prentice-Hall, Inc.
A Division of Simon & Schuster
Upper Saddle River, New Jersey 07458

PRENTICE HALL REGENTS
A VIACOM COMPANY

10 9 8 7 6 5 4 3 2 1

ISBN 0-13-359563-3

Prentice-Hall International (UK) Limited, *London*
Prentice-Hall of Australia Pty. Limited, *Sydney*
Prentice-Hall Canada Inc., *Toronto*
Prentice-Hall Hispanoamericana, S.A., *Mexico*
Prentice-Hall of India Private Limited, *New Delhi*
Prentice-Hall of Japan, Inc., *Tokyo*
Simon & Schuster Asia Pte. Ltd., *Singapore*
Editora Prentice-Hall do Brasil, Ltda., *Rio de Janeiro*

Molinsky, Steven J.
   Navigator 1 / Steven J. Molinsky, Bill Bliss.
       p. .cm.
   ISBN 0-13-359563-3
   1. English language—Textbooks for foreign speakers. 2. Li
skills—Problems, exercises, etc. 3. Readers—Life skills.
I. Molinsky, Steven J.   II. Title.
PE1128.B9287   95-5

Dear Teacher

Welcome to *Navigator* – our new English course in a unique magazine format. This five-level program offers adult and young-adult learners the competencies and content they need in order to function effectively in English. We have designed *Navigator* for use in a variety of learning situations: as a stand-alone course; as a supplement to *Side by Side*, *ExpressWays*, and other series; and as a motivating take-home text for students' independent learning and enjoyment.

We call ourselves a "text-zine" – part textbook, part magazine. Our goal is to offer a comprehensive English language syllabus in the non-traditional format of a popular magazine. We have tried to incorporate state-of-the-art instructional activities for active learning, cross-cultural exploration, problem-solving, and cooperative assessment as we offer students curriculum content that goes beyond lifeskills to include employment, the environment, technology, parenting, and other high-interest topics. Through the visual excitement of our page design and the diversity of magazine features that deliver the curriculum, we aim to create a learning experience for students that is lively, motivating, and fun.

NAVIGATOR FEATURES

Navigator offers you and your students these magazine features and departments:

Preview pages highlight each section's contents, offer photographs to activate students' prior knowledge and preview vocabulary and contexts, and provide a skills checklist students can use to assess their abilities before studying that section.

Conversations introduce vocabulary in the context of authentic communication that encourages lively conversation practice and role plays.

Navigator Asks pages offer on-the-street interviews that build vocabulary and encourage students to interview each other in class.

Discussion activities pose thought-provoking questions for students to answer in pairs, in small groups, and as a class.

Cultural Viewfinder activities stimulate learners to explore how people's living situations, attitudes, and behaviors are different in different cultures.

Did You Hear? listening practice pages include authentic tasks such as using voice-mail messaging services. (Listening scripts are at the back of the text.)

LifeWriter activities offer everyday writing experiences such as filling out applications and bank deposit slips.

Reading realia includes authentic reading material such as signs, labels, schedules, and directories.

Navigator Career Profiles feature interviews with real people who talk about their occupations.

Dear Navigator is our advice column, featuring letters that pose problems or questions about everyday life, culture, and customs.

Bulletin Boards contain brief notices with important information about key topics.

Stay in Shape Workouts get students moving around in fun "totally physical" action sequences for kinesthetic learning.

Contrasts pages present two photographs that stimulate students to reflect on situations, identify problems, and brainstorm solutions using a problem-posing approach.

Synthesizer activities present a breakthrough assessment alternative as students reflect on their knowledge and abilities and then work cooperatively in small groups and as a class to build teamwork skills.

WordChecker and **SkillChecker** lists enable students to do a quick self-assessment of their vocabulary acquisition and skill development.

Journal activities prompt students to record their experiences, ideas, and creative work in a personal composition book, so that they not only develop the necessary (but mundane) real-life writing skills they need for everyday life, but also develop their ability to write as a means of self-expression.

Puzzler Pages provide crosswords, word scrambles, funny license plates, and other activities for students' enjoyment.

WordRaps™ offer lively practice with pronunciation, rhythm, stress, and intonation.

SUGGESTED TEACHING STRATEGIES

We encourage you to use *Navigator* in a way that is compatible with your own teaching style and the needs and learning styles of your students. While no specific method or technique is required, we hope that you will use the materials to create a learning environment full of lively student interaction, lots of pair and group work, and rich opportunities for reflection, sharing, brainstorming, problem-solving, and creativity. Here are some suggestions you might want to try:

PREVIEW PAGE Using this opening page of each section, have students scan the list of features to preview the content of the section. Use the three photos and the accompanying preview questions to activate students' prior knowledge and to preview vocabulary and contexts. (You can also use each photo individually to preview a conversation on the day you introduce it, developing students' prediction skills as they describe the scene and guess what the people might be saying.) Have students look at the Skills Check statements and assess their abilities prior to studying the section.

CONVERSATIONS
1. *Previewing and Prediction:* Have students look at the photo for the conversation which appears on the Preview Page. Have them predict the situation and what the people might be saying. Then have students read the model conversation, decide if their predictions were correct, and discuss the situation.
2. *Listening:* With texts closed, have students listen to the model conversation – presented by you, by a pair of students, or on the audiotape. Check students' understanding of the situation and the vocabulary.

3. *Class Practice:* Have students repeat each line of the conversation chorally or individually.

4. *Pair Practice:* In pairs, have students practice the conversation.

5. *New Conversations:* Have pairs of students use the skeletal dialog and any exercises that may follow it to create new conversations based on the model. Pairs should practice and then take turns presenting the conversations to the class.

NAVIGATOR ASKS Have students practice the questions and answers in pairs, in small groups, or as a class. Check students' understanding of the vocabulary. Then have pairs of students create new conversations and present them to the class.

DISCUSSION ACTIVITIES Use these various activities (*Think About It, Talk About It, What's Your Opinion?, Person to Person,* and others) to promote student discussion in pairs, in small groups, and as a class. Build a true learning community in your classroom by encouraging students to share information about their backgrounds, their life experiences, their opinions, their plans and aspirations, and the other themes of these discussion activities.

CULTURAL VIEWFINDER Have students explore how cultures differ in people's living situations, attitudes, and behaviors. Ask students to reflect on their own experiences with cultural contrasts, and encourage them to share anecdotes and perceptions that illustrate the aspect of culture focused on in the lesson.

DID YOU HEAR? Have students complete these listening exercises as you play the audiotape or read from the listening script at the back of the text.

NAVIGATOR CAREER PROFILE Have students read the interview aloud in class, discuss their answers to the follow-up questions, and then do the activity that concludes the lesson. Have students also talk about whether they know anyone who works in the occupation, what kinds of skills and qualifications the occupation requires, and any other information they might want to learn about that type of work.

DEAR NAVIGATOR Use this advice column page to provoke thoughtful discussions about real-life situations and problems your students face. In pairs, in small groups, or as a class, have students read the first letter and the magazine's response. Then have them discuss their thoughts and feelings about the situation or problem, whether they agree or disagree with the magazine's advice, and how they might respond to the letter differently. (If your students work in pairs or small groups, leave enough time for them to also share their thoughts as a class.)

Then read the second letter together as a class. Have students think about a response to the letter individually, or develop their team-building skills by having them work in small groups to brainstorm ideas and reach a consensus about the best response. As a class, discuss students' suggestions for responses to the second letter. If time permits, encourage students to write their responses, exchange them with their classmates, and react to each other's ideas.

Finally, have students write their own *Dear Navigator* letters based on the questions posed by the text. Have them exchange letters with a classmate and write answers to each other's letters. In a later class session, have all students talk about their letters and the responses they received.

STAY IN SHAPE WORKOUT Use this activity to promote kinesthetic learning that helps students retain what they learn by attaching vocabulary and communication practice to lively and motivating action sequences. Have students look at the workout photographs and text and check their understanding of the vocabulary. Model for the class, or have students develop, a real action or a pantomime action that demonstrates each instruction. Give each instruction in sequence and have students act out the action. Then give the instructions in random sequence and have students act them out. Then have students practice in pairs, taking turns giving the instructions and acting them out. Finally, play "Workout Charades" as a class: have students take turns pantomiming an action as their classmates watch and call out the instruction.

CONTRASTS The two photos appear together to point out contrasts about life and the human condition – contrasts that may be sentimental, poignant, subtle, or stark. They are designed to provoke a reaction and to stimulate students to reflect on the situations depicted, the problems they pose, possible solutions, and applications to their own lives. These activities lend themselves to small group discussion followed by full class discussion. Use them to personalize the learning process for your students and to foster a learning community in which your students can share their thoughts and feelings and help each other identify problems and develop solutions.

SYNTHESIZER This activity helps your students consolidate what they have learned and helps you evaluate their progress. First, have students work individually to answer the questions posed at the top of the page. Then, have students work in small groups, sharing their individual responses to the questions and recording group members' responses on the chart. Finally, have students share as a class, tally class responses on the chart, and analyze the results. Encourage students to explore the reasons for their responses.

JOURNAL Encourage students to write their journal entries in a composition notebook – to keep as a record of their developing writing ability and their responses to the questions posed. If time permits, collect students' journals occasionally and write personal responses to their entries.

WORDRAPS™ Model these rhythm poems, have students present them chorally and individually, and encourage them to develop their own WordRaps™ based on the theme and beat of the originals.

We hope you and your students enjoy your journey through the pages of *Navigator*. Let us know what you think about our "text-zine". We'd love to hear from you.

Sincerely,

The Navigators

1 Getting to Know You

CONVERSATIONS

2 Nice to Meet You

4 What's Your Last Name?

8 How Are You?

PREVIEW

Look at these three pictures.
Who do you think these people are?
What's happening?
What are they saying to each other?

SKILLS CHECK

Can you . . .
- ☐ introduce yourself?
- ☐ talk about yourself?
- ☐ introduce family and friends?
- ☐ fill out forms?
- ☐ talk about what you want to learn?

Nice to Meet You

A. Hello. I'm Carlos.
B. Hi. My name's Tuan. Nice to meet you.
A. Nice to meet you, too. Where are you from?
B. Vietnam. How about you?
A. Mexico.

Practice with a partner. Introduce yourselves.

A. Hello. I'm _____.
B. Hi. My name's _____. Nice to meet you.
A. Nice to meet you, too. Where are you from?
B. _____. How about you?
A. _____.

YOU'RE ON THE MAP!

Use the map on page 3.
What country are you from? Put an X on your country.
What countries are your classmates from? Ask them.
Put a star (*) on each country.

A. What country are you from?
B. _____.
A. Where is it?
B. It's right here.

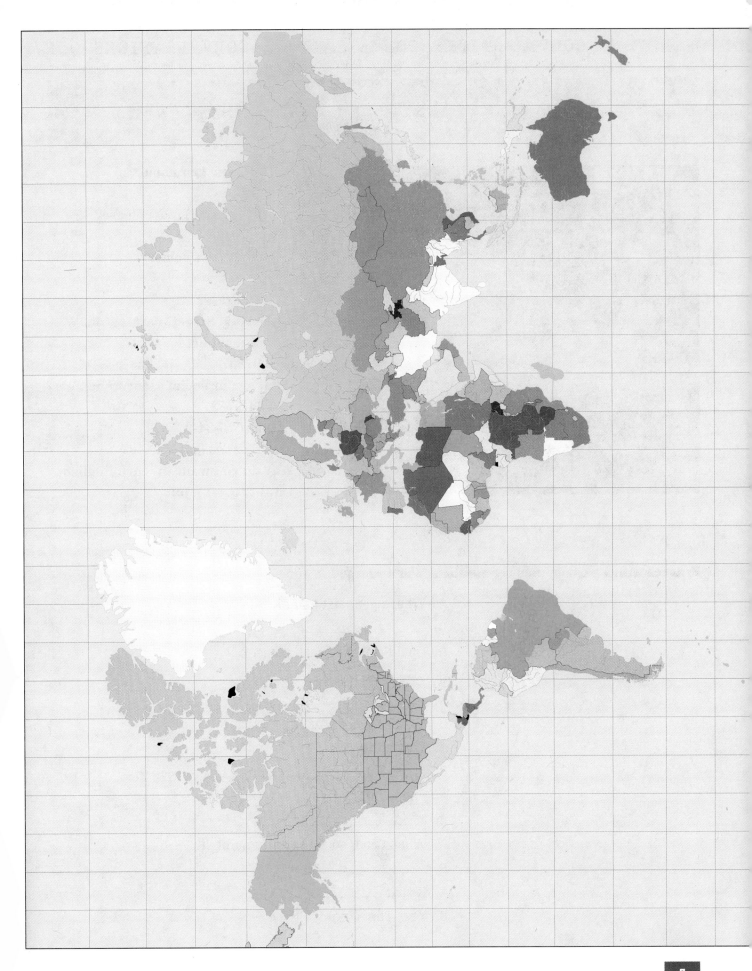

What's Your Last Name?

A. What's your last name?
B. Han.
A. Could you spell that, please?
B. H - A - N.
A. And your first name?
B. Mai.
A. Your address?
B. 1020 Allen Street, Parkington.
A. Phone number?
B. 672–9783.
A. What's your social security number?
B. 076-34-9783.
A. Is that 076-34-9783?
B. Yes. That's right.
A. Why do you want to learn English?
B. I want to get a job.

Practice with a partner. Answer questions about yourself.

A. What's your last name?
B. _____ .
A. Could you spell that, please?
B. _____ .
A. And your first name?
B. _____ .
A. Your address?
B. _____ .
A. Phone number?
B. _____ .
A. What's your social security number?
B. _____ .
A. Is that _____ ?
B. Yes. That's right.

Interview

Interview your classmates. Ask about names and countries. Ask something else you want to know. Write the information on the chart.

A. What's your last name?
B. _____.
A. How do you spell that?
B. _____.
A. What's your first name?
B. _____.
A. How do you spell that?
B. _____.
A. Where are you from?
B. _____.
A. _____?
B. _____.

LAST NAME	FIRST NAME	COUNTRY	_____ your question

NAVIGATOR asks:

Why do you want to learn English?

I want to *speak English at the bank.*

I want to *go to college.*

get a job

get a better job

get job training

help my children with school

go to school meetings

write notes

talk to my landlord

rent an apartment

buy a house

speak English at the clinic

speak English at the post office

speak English in stores

use the bus

use the subway system

understand signs

buy a car

understand contracts

read my mail

read English language newspapers

understand the news

become a citizen

Practice conversations with a partner. Use all the reasons on pages 6 and 7.

A. Why do you want to learn English?

B. I want to _____.

PERSON TO PERSON

Talk with a partner. Then share as a class. Why do YOU want to learn English?

WHAT'S YOUR OPINION?

Why is it important to learn English? Discuss in pairs or small groups. Then share as a class.

How Are You?

A. Hi, Karen. How are you?
B. Fine. And you?
A. Fine, thanks. Karen, this is my husband, Daniel.
B. Nice to meet you, Daniel.
C. Nice to meet you, too.

Practice in groups of three. Introduce family members and friends.

A. Hi, _____. How are you?
B. Fine. And you?
A. Fine, thanks. _____, this is my _____, _____.
B. Nice to meet you, _____.
C. Nice to meet you, too.

❶ wife, Shirley

❷ father, Mr. Wong

❸ mother, Mrs. Chen

❹ son, Peter

❺ daughter, Jessica

❻ friend, Alex

YOUR PHOTO ALBUM

Draw pictures or bring in photographs of your family or friends.
Tell a classmate about each person. Then tell the class.

Did You Hear?

WHAT'S YOUR TELEPHONE NUMBER?
Listen and circle the numbers you hear.

1	567–3489	(462–8934)	5	524	934
2	786–2165	876–1256	6	305	1135
3	237–1324	237–1234	7	4209	1429
4	1015	215	8	1330	1313

COULD YOU SPELL THAT, PLEASE?
Listen and fill in the missing letters.

1	S _m_ i t h	5	P __ t e __ s
2	C __ r l o s	6	T __ __ y
3	T u a __	7	__ l __ __ n
4	A __ d u l	8	__ __ __ __ __ __ __

WHAT'S YOUR LAST NAME?
Listen to the question and circle the correct answer.

1	(Smith)	Apartment 3B	5	Ed Stuart	21 Elm Street
2	358–4213	Martinez	6	351–2456	15A
3	315	433–2970	7	687–23–6402	549–2360
4	#14D	247–9318	8	(703) 549–2074	934–28–6075

LIFEWRITER

REGISTRATION FORMS

Life is full of forms. Can you fill these out?

Name _____
    First   Last

Address _____
        Number   Street
        _____
        City   State   Zip Code

Telephone _____ _____
          Area Code   Number

Social Security Number _____   **FOR OFFICIAL USE ONLY**

Marital Status: M _____
                  S _____

Name Last ☐☐☐☐☐☐☐☐☐☐☐☐☐☐ First ☐☐☐☐☐☐☐☐☐☐☐☐☐☐☐☐☐

Address ☐☐☐☐☐☐☐☐☐☐☐☐☐☐☐☐☐☐☐☐☐☐☐☐☐☐☐☐☐☐☐☐☐☐
           Number   Street
           ☐☐☐☐☐☐☐☐☐☐☐☐☐☐☐☐☐ ☐☐   ☐☐☐☐☐
           City   State   Zip Code

Telephone ☐☐☐ ☐☐☐☐☐☐☐   **Married** ☐
                                          Single ☐

Social Security Number ☐☐☐ ☐☐ ☐☐☐☐

Why do you want to study English?

_____

_____

NAVIGATOR CAREER PROFILE

Deborah Schaffer, ESL Teacher

Q: What's your name?
A: Deborah Schaffer.

Q: Where are you from?
A: New York. But now I live in Virginia.

Q: What do you do?
A: I'm an ESL teacher. I teach English.

Q: Where are your students from?
A: They're from North America, Central America, South America, Africa, Asia, and Europe.

Q: Your students are from all over the world!
A: That's right.

Q: What do you like about your job?
A: I like people. I like to help people. And I like to teach.

YOU'RE THE INTERVIEWER!

Do a magazine profile. Interview your teacher or someone else. Write your answers in your reporter's notebook.

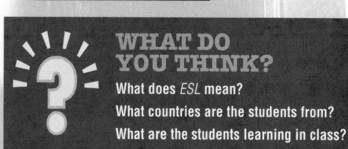

WHAT DO YOU THINK?

What does *ESL* mean?
What countries are the students from?
What are the students learning in class?

Q. What's your name?

A. _____.

Q. Where are you from?

A. _____.

Q. What do you do?

A. _____.

Q. _____?

A. _____.

Q. What do you like about your job?

A. _____.

Dear Navigator

Dear Navigator,

I am happy and sad. I'm happy because I go to school to learn English. I'm sad because I don't understand many things in my class.

I feel stupid. I feel like a child. Maybe I'm too old to learn English. What do you think?

Sincerely,

Happy and Sad in L.A.

Dear Happy and Sad in L.A.,

You are not too old to learn English! Don't worry. Many students feel like this. Ask questions. Ask for help. Your teacher will be happy to help you.

Good luck!

Sincerely,

Navigator

Dear Navigator,

My English teacher's name is Fred Lang. I call my teacher "Mr. Lang." My teacher says, "Please call me Fred." But I can't. He's my teacher. In my country, we don't use a teacher's first name. So now I call my teacher Mr. Fred. Is this okay?

Sincerely,

New Student in Miami

Readers: What's your English teacher's name? What do you call your English teacher? In your culture do you use a teacher's first name? What do you call a teacher? Discuss this with other students. Then answer *New Student in Miami's* letter.

Dear New Student in Miami,

_____

_____

_____

Sincerely,

_____

Titles:

Ms.
Miss } for a woman
Mrs.

Mr.   for a man

Dr.   for a doctor

Now write your own Dear Navigator letter.

Describe how you feel about English and school. What don't you understand about English? What don't you understand about life in this country? Exchange letters with a classmate, and write answers to each other's letters. Then share with the class.

STAY IN SHAPE WITH THE
Personal Information WORKOUT

1 Stand up.

2 Go to the board.

3 Write your name.

4 Sit down.

5 Stand up.

6 Go to the board.

Sit down. **8**

Write your address. **7**

Stand up. **9**

Erase your name. **11**

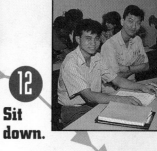

12 Sit down.

10 Go to the board.

13 Stand up.

Sit down. **16**

15

Erase your address.

14 Go to the board.

Navigator 1

13

CONTRASTS
Families

Look at the photos. What are you thinking? What are you feeling?
What differences do you see?
Do you see any problems? What are the solutions?
Reflect on your own, discuss in pairs or in small groups, and share as a class.

SYNTHESIZER

Why do you want to learn English? Write five reasons.

COOPERATIVE TEAM • INFORMATION SKILLS
Acquiring
Organizing
Communicating
Analyzing

_____

_____

_____

_____

_____

**In small groups, share the reasons you want to learn English. Fill in the chart
for your group. Write the reasons. Write the number of students for each reason.**

REASONS	Your Group	Another Group	Another Group	Another Group	Another Group	Class Total

**Now share as a class. Report your group's results. Fill in the other
groups' results on the chart. Add up the numbers of students. In your
class, what are the _top five_ reasons students want to learn English?**

_____   _____

_____   _____

_____

WordChecker

name
first name
last name
address
phone number
social security
  number
Hello
Hi

husband
wife
father
mother
son
daughter
friend

SkillChecker

I can . . .
☐ introduce myself
☐ talk about myself
☐ introduce family and
  friends
☐ fill out forms
☐ talk about what I want
  to learn

JOURNAL

Write a short autobiography
in your Navigator Journal.

What's your name?
What's your address?
What country are you from?
Why do you want to learn
  English?

PUZZLER PAGE

EZ 4 U?
Can you read the license plates?

CALIFORNIA
HOW R U

FLORIDA
I M FINE

NEW YORK
C U L8R

DESCRAMBLER

Unscramble the words. Then use the circled letters to make a new word and finish the sentence.

1. f r e t h a   f a (t) h e r
2. t a g u h r e d   (○) _ _ _ _ _ _ _
3. s h u n b a d   _ (○) _ _ _ _ _
4. t e r s s i   (○) _ (○) _ _ _
5. b o r r h e t   _ _ _ _ _ (○) _
6. f e w i   _ (○) _ _

What does Carlos do every night?

He _ _ _ _ _ _ _ _.

WORDRAP™

Nice to Meet You

JILL: Hi. I'm Jill.
BILL: Hello. I'm Bill.
JILL: Nice to meet you.
BILL: Nice to meet you.

JILL: Bill, this is Phil.
BILL: Hi, Phil. I'm Bill.
PHIL: Nice to meet you.
BILL: Nice to meet you.

ANN: Hi. I'm Ann.
FRAN: Hello. I'm Fran.
ANN: Nice to meet you.
FRAN: Nice to meet you.

ANN: Fran, this is Dan.
FRAN: Hi, Dan. I'm Fran.
DAN: Nice to meet you.
FRAN: Nice to meet you.

Now write your own raps with names that rhyme.

WordSearcher
Can you find the words?

```
S T (N U M B E R) O T
Z P O F I P W N H E
H Y E A A C L X R L
H U Z L Y O N A M E
X V J B L U P V L P
O G G S M N D P N H
X V W H A T B B E O
L V D L B R P O O N
W H E R E Y O O J E
A D D R E S S I M S
```

NUMBER   TELEPHONE
COUNTRY   WHERE
SPELL   WHAT
ADDRESS   NAME

Making a Living

CONVERSATIONS

18 **What Kind of Job Do You Want?**

20 **How's Your Work Schedule?**

21 **Watch Out!**

PREVIEW

Look at these three pictures.

Who do you think these people are?

What's happening?

What are they saying to each other?

YOUR EMPLOYABILITY CHECKUP

Can you . . .
- [ ] *name occupations?*
- [ ] *describe your job needs?*
- [ ] *describe your skills?*
- [ ] *scan and read Help Wanted ads?*
- [ ] *fill out a job application form?*
- [ ] *tell time?*
- [ ] *read a work schedule?*
- [ ] *fill out a timesheet?*
- [ ] *use short emergency warnings?*
- [ ] *read warning signs?*

What Kind of Job Do You Want?

A. What kind of job do you want?

B. I want a job as a painter.

A. Tell me about your skills.

B. I can use a spray gun, and I can mix paint.

A. What kind of work did you do before?

B. I was a farmer.

Practice with a partner. Talk about jobs you want.

A. What kind of job do you want?

B. I want a job as _____.

A. Tell me about your skills.

B. I can _____, and I can _____.

1 a cashier
use a cash register
handle money

2 a secretary
type
file

3 an electrician
install light fixtures
wire a house

4 a waiter
take orders
serve customers

5 a medical technician
take a blood sample
do lab tests

Now practice conversations about other jobs and skills. Present your conversations to the class.

Interview

Interview some classmates.
Ask about their work experience.
Write the information on the chart.

A. What kind of work did you do before?

B. I was a/an _____.

NAME	PREVIOUS EXPERIENCE
_____	_____
_____	_____
_____	_____
_____	_____

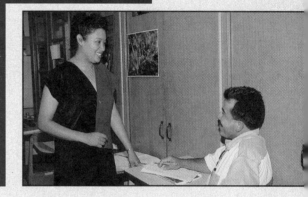

Interview some other classmates. Ask about their skills. Write sentences on the chart.

A. Tell me about your skills.

B. I can _____, and _____.

SKILLS

NAME

_____ can _____ and _____.
_____ can _____ and _____.
_____ can _____ and _____.
_____ can _____ and _____.
_____ can _____ and _____.

JOB-HUNTING STRATEGIES

What are some good ways to look for jobs in your area? Brainstorm with a partner. Then share your ideas as a class.

How's Your Work Schedule?

Sun	Mon	Tues	Wed	Thur	Fri	Sat
✔	✔	✔		✔	✔	✔

A. How's your work schedule for next week?
B. It's okay.
A. When are you off?
B. I'm off on Wednesday.

Practice with a partner. Talk about days off.

A. How's your work schedule for next week?
B. It's okay.
A. When are you off?
B. I'm off on _____.

1

2

3

4

5

6

WHAT DO YOU THINK?

Where do you see schedules at school? at work? in the community? Why are schedules important?

CULTURAL VIEWFINDER

Compare work schedules in different countries you know. How are the schedules similar or different? Do people follow the schedules?

Watch Out!

**Practice with a partner.
Give warnings.**

A. Watch out!
B. Excuse me?
A. The floor is wet.
B. Thanks.

A. _____!
B. Excuse me?
A. _____!
B. Thanks.

1 Watch out!
Don't stand there.

2 Be careful!
You need a helmet.

3 Look out!
Don't touch that.

4 Careful!
You need safety glasses.

5 Watch out!
There's wet paint.

6 Careful!
Don't go that way.

SAFETY FIRST!
Draw some safety signs you see at school, at work, or on the street.

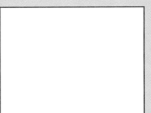

Navigator 1 21

Did You Hear?

WHAT'S THE WARNING SIGN?
Listen to the warnings and check the correct sign.

1  ✓

2

3

4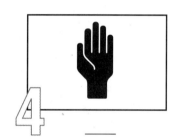

5 EMERGENCY EXIT ONLY

6

WHAT'S THE WORK SCHEDULE?
Listen to the conversations about schedules. Circle the day you hear.

1	(Monday)	Wednesday	4	Tuesday	Wednesday
2	Friday	Thursday	5	Sunday	Monday
3	Saturday	Sunday	6	Thursday	Tuesday

LIFEWRITER

JOB APPLICATION FORM

You're looking for a job. Can you complete the form? Give information about your work experience.

Name: _____ Social Security No. _____
      Last   First   M.I.

Address: _____
         Number   Street   Telephone _____

_____
City   State   Zip Code   Are you 18 or older?   Yes ☐   No ☐

Work Experience

Job Title
                                        From   To

1. _____

2. _____

3. _____

4. _____

5. _____

6. _____

   _____

_____
Signature
                        _____
                        Date

Carry this page when you go to apply for a job. The information about your work experience is important.

It's About Time!

| *eight* o'clock | *eight* fifteen
a quarter after *eight* | *eight* thirty
half past *eight* | *eight* forty-five
a quarter to *nine* |

A. What time is it?
B. It's eight o'clock.

Practice telling time with a partner.

A. What time is it?
B. It's _____.

CARMEN'S WORK SCHEDULE
Read Carmen's work schedule and answer the questions.

S = Start   **E = End**

NAME		11/27	11/28	11/29	11/30	12/01	12/02	12/03
		SUN	MON	TUES	WED	THUR	FRI	SAT
Lopez, C	S	12:00 PM	8:30 AM	8:30 AM		9:15 AM	9:15 AM	7:45 AM
	E	9:00 PM	2:30 PM	2:30 PM		6:15 PM	6:15 PM	4:45 PM

1 How many days does Carmen work this week?

2 Which day is her day off?

3 What time does she start work on Tuesday?

4 What time does she start work on Saturday?

5 What time does she leave work on Monday?

6 What time does she leave work on Friday?

7 What day does she leave at 9:00?

8 How many hours does she work on Sunday?

9 How many hours does she work on Tuesday?

10 What is the total number of hours she works this week?

Months of the Year

January
February
March
April
May
June
July
August
September
October
November
December

IT'S A DATE!

Say the Date	Write the Date
August twentieth, nineteen ninety-nine	August 20, 1999 8/20/99

Write these dates as numbers and practice saying them.

February 21, 1998   _2/21/98_   January 1, 1997   _____

December 11, 1927   _____   November 16, 2000   _____

July 4, 1976   _____   March 8, 1967   _____

May 29, 1946   _____   June 30, 1987   _____

YOUR TIME SHEET

In many workplaces, people fill out a timesheet every two weeks. Fill out this timesheet with your work hours or your English class hours.

Ordinal Numbers

first
second
third
fourth
fifth
sixth
seventh
eighth
ninth
tenth
eleventh
twelfth
thirteenth
fourteenth
fifteenth
sixteenth
seventeenth
eighteenth
nineteenth
twentieth
twenty-first
thirtieth
thirty-first

Employee Name _____

Pay Period from _____ to _____

Date	Time In	Time Out	Total Hours

Total hours _____

Signature _____   Date _____

Navigator Classifieds

These people are looking for jobs. Read the sentences about their job skills. Then decide which Help Wanted ad describes a job for each person.

_C_	1	Liz can drive a car and a bus.
____	2	Brenda can clean rooms and make beds.
____	3	Roberto can handle money and use a cash register.
____	4	Amy can do lab tests and take blood.
____	5	Tony can bake bread and cakes.
____	6	Sonia can cook pizza and make pasta.
____	7	Bill can type and file.
____	8	Yasmin can keep records and work with numbers.
____	9	Tuan can install light fixtures.

HELP WANTED

BAKER [a]
Part time. No experience required. Will train. Apply in person. Royal Pastry Shop, 340 Main St.

Bookkeeper for small office. Full-time. Call Vanessa at 497–3321. [b]

Bus drivers [c]
Greenfield Public School system needs experienced drivers. Call Mrs. Hunt at 738–5419.

Cashiers — Large supermarket. Full-time and part-time. Apply at 1200 Central Avenue. [d]

Cook — Pizza Shack needs cook 4 hours/day. Apply 2:00 - 4:00 P.M. Green Street & River Road. [e]

Electrician's Assistant [f]
Need tools and transportation. Call 415–627–9913.

Now taking applications for [g]
Housekeepers
New hotel seeks housekeepers. Experience not necessary. Palace Hotel, 2920 Broadway. Mon – Fri, 10 – 6. No phone calls, please.

Medical technician. Take blood. Do lab tests. 2+ years experience. Contact Sue at 858–1837. [h]

Secretary Downtown office. Type and file. Call Mark at 591–7020. [i]

Part-time. No experience nec-
Call Dave at 561-7423.

Classified Information!

There's a lot of information in these Help Wanted ads.
Can you find the information you need to answer these questions?

1 Which jobs are full-time?
_____

2 Which jobs are part-time?
_____

3 Which jobs don't require experience?
_____

4 Which jobs do you apply for in person?
_____

5 Which jobs do you call about?
_____

NAVIGATOR CAREER PROFILE

Antonio Soto, Painter

Q: What's your name?
A: Antonio Soto.

Q: Where are you from?
A: Bolivia.

Q: What did you do in your country?
A: I was an engineer.

Q: What do you do now?
A: I'm a painter, and I study English at night.

Q: What do you do in your job?
A: I paint houses. I paint offices. I paint buildings inside and outside.

Q: How did you get your job?
A: My friend helped me.

Q: What do you like about your job?
A: I like to work with my hands, and I like to make things look new.

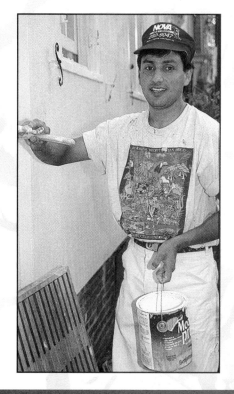

YOU'RE THE INTERVIEWER!

Do a magazine profile. Interview another student or someone else you know. Write your answers in your reporter's notebook. Then do a presentation for the class about this person.

WHAT DO YOU THINK?

Antonio was an engineer in his country. Why isn't he an engineer now? How does he feel about this? How is he preparing for the future? Is your situation like Antonio's? How?

Q. What's your name?
A. _____.

Q. Where are you from?
A. _____.

Q. What's your occupation?
A. _____.

Q. What do you do in your job?
A. _____.

Q. How did you get your job?
A. _____.

Q. What do you like about your job?
A. _____.

Dear Navigator

Dear Navigator,

In my country I worked in my family's business. Now I am alone here. I want to work, but I don't know how to find a job, and my English isn't very good. Can you help me?

Sincerely,

Jobless in Seattle

Dear Jobless in Seattle,

There are many ways to find jobs. Ask friends. Look for Help Wanted signs in store windows. Look for job announcements on bulletin boards in supermarkets. Read the classified ads in your local newspaper. Go to the public employment office in your community. And study English! Take an ESL class that teaches English for work.

Good luck!

Sincerely,

Navigator

Dear Navigator,

In Afghanistan, I was a chemical engineer. Now I'm in the United States, and I'm a taxi driver. I want to work in my profession, but it's very difficult.

I don't know English very well. I go to ESL classes sometimes, but I can't go to school very much. I drive my taxi at night. During the day, my wife cleans houses and I watch our baby. My family needs the money.

I want a good life for my family. But I'm very worried about the future. What can I do?

Sincerely,

Cab Driver in Brooklyn

Readers: What's your opinion about *Cab Driver in Brooklyn's* problem? Discuss this with other students. Then answer the letter.

Dear Cab Driver in Brooklyn,

_____

_____

_____

_____

Sincerely,

_____

Now write your own
Dear Navigator letter.

Describe how you feel about work and your future. Exchange letters with a classmate, and write answers to each other's letters. Then share with the class.

STAY IN SHAPE WITH THE
Help Wanted WORKOUT

1 Pick up a newspaper.

2 Open the paper to the classified ads.

3 Find the Help Wanted section.

4 Scan the ads.

5 Find a job you like.

6 Circle the ad.

7 Write down the number.

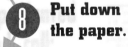

8 Put down the paper.

9 Go to the phone.

10 Dial the number.

11 Apply for the job.

CITY OF LOS ANGELES

DAY LABORER·PROGRAM

EAST VALLEY SITE

CIUDAD DE LOS ANGELES

PROGRAMA DE TRABAJADORES POR DIA

LOCAL DEL ESTE DEL VALLE

| MONDAY THRU SATURDAY. 6 AM TO 2 NOON |
| TELEPHONE 503-8842 OR 503-9006 |

WORK WANTED

CONTRASTS
Applying for a Job

Look at the photos. What are you thinking? What are you feeling?
What are the situations? What differences do you see?
Do you see any problems? What are the solutions?
Reflect on your own, discuss in pairs or in small groups, and share as a class.

SYNTHESIZER

Answer these questions.

Did you work before you started
this English course? ☐ Yes ☐ No

Do you work now? ☐ Yes ☐ No

Do you like your work? ☐ Yes ☐ No

How many hours do you work in one week? _____

In small groups, talk about your answers to these questions. Fill in the chart for your group. Write the number of students on each line.

HOW MANY STUDENTS	Your Group	Another Group	Another Group	Another Group	Another Group	Class Total
worked before?						
work now?						
like work?						
don't like work?						
average student's hours of work per week						

Now share as a class. Report your group's results. Fill in the other groups' results on the chart. Add up the numbers of students. Then *analyze* the information about your class. Do you see anything interesting about students and their work? Discuss with other students.

WordChecker

baker
bookkeeper
bus driver
cashier
cook
electrician
electrician's
  assistant
engineer
farmer
housekeeper
medical
  technician
painter
secretary
waiter

application form
classified ad
day off
timesheet
work experience
work schedule
Be careful!
Careful!
Look out!
Watch out!
Days of the
  week
Months of the
  year

SkillChecker

I can . . .
☐ name occupations
☐ describe my job needs
☐ describe my skills
☐ scan and read Help
  Wanted ads
☐ fill out a job application
  form
☐ tell time
☐ read a work schedule
☐ fill out a timesheet
☐ use short emergency
  warnings
☐ read warning signs

JOURNAL

Write a paragraph about the job you have or the job you want.

What job is it?

What do you do in this job?

What kind of education do you need?

In your opinion, is this a good job? Why?

PUZZLER PAGE

CLOSE-UP

What's the object?
Who uses it at work?

DESCRAMBLER

Unscramble these words about safety at work. Then use the circled letters to make a new word and finish the sentence.

1. g a n d r e   d a n g e r
2. a r e f l u c   ⃝ _ _ ⃝ _ _ _
3. s l a s g e s   ⃝ _ _ _ _ _ _
4. s t e f a y   _ _ _ _ _ ⃝
5. t h l e m e   _ ⃝ _ ⃝ _ _

Use this exit only in an

_ _ _ _ _ _ _ _ _ _ .

EZ 4 U?

Can you read the license plate?

CALIFORNIA
IMA W8R

Crossword

1 W	O	R	K			2			

Across
1. The _____ schedule lists our hours and days off.
3. A _____ paints houses.
5. Write your hours on the _____.
6. A _____ types and files.

Down
1. A _____ serves food.
2. A _____ handles money in a store.
4. I _____ a job.

WORDRAP™

A Terrible Place to Work!
Don't apply
   for a job in that place.
It's a terrible place
   to work!
The hours are long.
The breaks are short.
The pay is poor.
The boss is mean.
The people are nasty.
The work is dull.
It's a terrible place
   to work!

A Wonderful Place to Work!
You should apply
   for a job in that place.
It's a wonderful place
   to work!
The hours are short.
The breaks are long.
The pay is good.
The boss is kind.
The people are nice.
The work is fun.
It's a wonderful place
   to work!

3 Food Shopping

CONVERSATIONS

34 I'm Making a Shopping List

35 Where Are the Eggs?/Where's the Juice?

37 That'll Be $3.79

PREVIEW

Look at these three pictures.

Who do you think these people are?

What's happening?

What are they saying to each other?

SKILLS CHECK

Can you . . .

☐ *describe your food needs?*
☐ *make a shopping list?*
☐ *locate items in the supermarket?*
☐ *order fast food?*
☐ *pay for food and get change?*
☐ *fill out a rebate coupon?*

I'm Making a Shopping List

A. I'm making a shopping list. What do we need?
B. We need eggs.
A. Okay. Anything else?
B. Yes. We need butter.

Practice with a partner. Tell what you need from the supermarket. Make shopping lists.

A. I'm making a shopping list. What do we need?
B. We need _____.
A. Okay. Anything else?
B. Yes. We need _____.

tomatoes

apples

eggs

cheese

rice

bread

lettuce

milk

ice cream

coffee

chicken

THINK ABOUT IT
What other kinds of lists do people make?

Where Are the Eggs?

STORE DIRECTORY	
APPLES	2
EGGS	3
ONIONS	1
PAPER PRODUCTS	9
SOFT DRINKS	7
TOMATOES	1

A. Excuse me. Where are the eggs?
B. They're in aisle 3.

Practice with a partner. Locate these items in the supermarket.

A. Excuse me. Where are the _____?
B. They're in aisle _____.

Where's the Juice?

STORE DIRECTORY	
BREAD	10
CHEESE	3
CHICKEN	4
JUICE	5
LETTUCE	1
MILK	3

A. Excuse me. Where's the juice?
B. It's in aisle 5.

Practice with a partner. Locate these items in the supermarket.

A. Excuse me. Where's the _____?
B. It's in aisle _____.

NAVIGATOR goes behind the counter and asks:
Are you ready to order?

I'd like *a cheeseburger, small fries, and a medium Coke.*

a hamburger, large fries, and a small coffee

a chicken sandwich, a small salad, and milk

two tacos, beans, and a large lemonade

a fish sandwich, medium fries, and a small chocolate shake

a burrito, rice, and a medium Pepsi

a number three meal with an iced tea

Practice conversations with a partner. Order these meals and others.

A. Are you ready to order?

B. I'd like _____.

That'll Be $3.79

A. That'll be $3.79.
B. $3.79? Here you are.
A. Out of $5.00. Your change is $1.21.
B. Thanks.
A. Have a nice day.

Practice with a partner. Pay for food and get your change.

A. That'll be _____.
B. _____? Here you are.
A. Out of _____. Your change is _____.
B. Thanks.
A. Have a nice day.

1
Total	4.59
Cash	5.00
Change	.41

2
Total	7.45
Cash	10.00
Change	2.55

3
Total	1.98
Cash	5.00
Change	3.02

4
Total	_____
Cash	_____
Change	_____

PERSON TO PERSON
Place your order with a partner. Compute the total and any change.

A. Are you ready to order?
B. I'd like _____.
A. That'll be _____.
B. _____? Here you are.
A. Out of _____. Your change is _____.
B. Thanks.
A. Have a nice day.

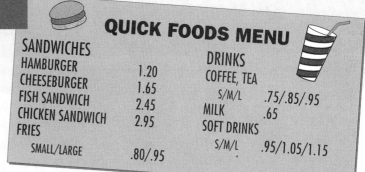

QUICK FOODS MENU

SANDWICHES
HAMBURGER 1.20
CHEESEBURGER 1.65
FISH SANDWICH 2.45
CHICKEN SANDWICH 2.95
FRIES
SMALL/LARGE .80/.95

DRINKS
COFFEE, TEA
S/M/L .75/.85/.95
MILK .65
SOFT DRINKS
S/M/L .95/1.05/1.15

WHAT'S YOUR OPINION?
Is it a good idea to eat in fast-food restaurants?

Did You Hear?

THAT'LL BE $4.89
Listen to the cashier. Circle the amount you hear.

1	$3.29	($ 4.89)	5	$67.43	$76.34
2	$5.32	$ 9.22	6	$54.67	$24.47
3	$2.98	$10.89	7	$16.73	$70.16
4	$8.47	$ 7.40	8	$14.92	$40.92

ARE YOU READY TO ORDER?

Listen to each customer. Put a check next to the item each customer orders. Circle S, M, or L for sizes of drinks — small, medium, or large.

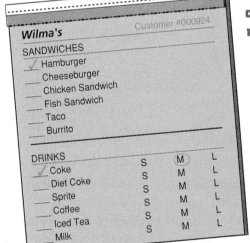

1

Wilma's   Customer #000924

SANDWICHES
- ✓ Hamburger
- ___ Cheeseburger
- ___ Chicken Sandwich
- ___ Fish Sandwich
- ___ Taco
- ___ Burrito

DRINKS
- ✓ Coke   S   (M)   L
- ___ Diet Coke   S   M   L
- ___ Sprite   S   M   L
- ___ Coffee   S   M   L
- ___ Iced Tea   S   M   L
- ___ Milk   S   M   L

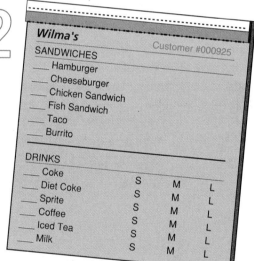

2

Wilma's   Customer #000925

SANDWICHES
- ___ Hamburger
- ___ Cheeseburger
- ___ Chicken Sandwich
- ___ Fish Sandwich
- ___ Taco
- ___ Burrito

DRINKS
- ___ Coke   S   M   L
- ___ Diet Coke   S   M   L
- ___ Sprite   S   M   L
- ___ Coffee   S   M   L
- ___ Iced Tea   S   M   L
- ___ Milk   S   M   L

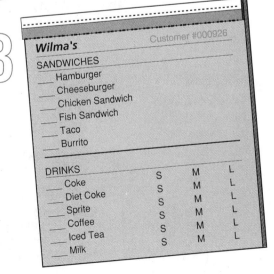

3

Wilma's   Customer #000926

SANDWICHES
- ___ Hamburger
- ___ Cheeseburger
- ___ Chicken Sandwich
- ___ Fish Sandwich
- ___ Taco
- ___ Burrito

DRINKS
- ___ Coke   S   M   L
- ___ Diet Coke   S   M   L
- ___ Sprite   S   M   L
- ___ Coffee   S   M   L
- ___ Iced Tea   S   M   L
- ___ Milk   S   M   L

4

Wilma's   Customer #000927

SANDWICHES
- ___ Hamburger
- ___ Cheeseburger
- ___ Chicken Sandwich
- ___ Fish Sandwich
- ___ Taco
- ___ Burrito

DRINKS
- ___ Coke   S   M   L
- ___ Diet Coke   S   M   L
- ___ Sprite   S   M   L
- ___ Coffee   S   M   L
- ___ Iced Tea   S   M   L
- ___ Milk   S   M   L

LIFEWRITER

SHOPPING LISTS

People often make lists to help them remember what they have to do. What's on this person's shopping list?

Shopping List

List of Ingredients

**What's your favorite meal?
What ingredients do you need
to prepare it?**

REBATE COUPONS

You can save money with rebate coupons. Get the coupon at the supermarket. Coupons are on the shelves, at the checkout counter, or on the wall. Fill in the coupon, cut out the UPC symbol on the product, and circle the product on the receipt. Here's one coupon for practice.

```
JUMBO SUPERMARKET          #473
   LARGE EGGS              1.15
4@$1.25
   SWAN SOAP               5.00
BAKING POWDER              1.49
               CASH    20.00
               CHANGE  12.36
   Thanks for shopping JUMBO
```

receipt

circle the item

UPC symbol

D325 9041

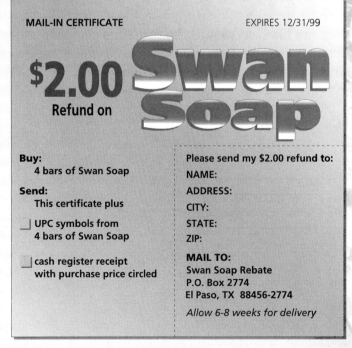

MAIL-IN CERTIFICATE   EXPIRES 12/31/99

$2.00 Refund on   **Swan Soap**

Buy:
4 bars of Swan Soap

Send:
This certificate plus

☐ UPC symbols from
4 bars of Swan Soap

☐ cash register receipt
with purchase price circled

Please send my $2.00 refund to:
NAME:
ADDRESS:
CITY:
STATE:
ZIP:

MAIL TO:
Swan Soap Rebate
P.O. Box 2774
El Paso, TX 88456-2774

Allow 6-8 weeks for delivery

NAVIGATOR Goes Food Shopping

Supermarket Sections

Supermarkets are very large these days. The typical supermarket has lots of items in many sections. Go to your supermarket. List items in each of these sections.

Bakery: _____bread_____

_____

_____

_____

Meat: _____beef_____

_____

_____

_____

Paper Products: _____tissues_____

_____

_____

_____

Dairy: _____milk_____

_____

_____

_____

Produce: _____apples_____

_____

_____

_____

Frozen Foods: _____ice cream_____

_____

_____

_____

Where's the Soy Sauce?

You can't find an item at the supermarket. Find the store directory. It lists the supermarket sections and their locations. Here are some food items. Where can you find them? Write the aisle numbers.

		Aisle				Aisle
1	milk	6		7	ice cream	___
2	onions	___		8	toilet paper	___
3	oranges	___		9	tomato sauce	___
4	napkins	___		10	beef	___
5	cake	___		11	yogurt	___
6	canned peaches	___		12	soy sauce	___

STORE DIRECTORY

	AISLE
BAKERY	10
CANNED GOODS	3
DAIRY PRODUCTS	6
FROZEN FOOD	9
INTERNATIONAL	11
JUICE	2
MEAT	5
PAPER PRODUCTS	7
PRODUCE	1
SOAP	8
SOUP	3
SPICES	4

On the Supermarket Wall

What are the reasons for these rules?

Welcome, customers!

We ask for your cooperation.

No smoking.
Shirts and shoes required.
No pets.
Don't open packages.
Watch your purse and belongings.
Don't leave children unattended.
Lock your car.
Don't remove shopping carts from the parking lot.

Thank you for shopping at Jumbo Supermarket!

Wanda Jackson
STORE MANAGER

Read the ads. Then write an ad and post it on the supermarket bulletin board.

FREE AD

Name: _Carmen_   Date: _5/24_

_Dining room table and
6 chairs for sale.
Good condition._

IMPORTANT Write your telephone number in the spaces below
Phone 267-1128
Phone 267-1128
Phone 267-1128
Phone 267-1128
Phone 267-1128

FREE AD

Name: _Quong_   Date: _6/3_

_Housecleaning, gardening,
odd jobs._

IMPORTANT Write your telephone number in the spaces below
Phone 265-7341
Phone 265-7341
Phone 265-7341
Phone 265-7341
Phone 265-7341

FREE AD

Name: _Natalya_   Date: _5/31_

Will babysit in your home.

IMPORTANT Write your telephone number in the spaces below
Phone 543-9702
Phone 543-9702
Phone 543-9702
Phone 543-9702
Phone 543-9702

FREE AD

Name: _____   Date: _____

IMPORTANT Write your telephone number in the spaces below
Phone
Phone
Phone
Phone
Phone

What kind of ads are on the bulletin board at your supermarket? Copy some and share with your class.

Navigator Eats Lunch!

The Navigator staff is ordering lunch from the Lunch Time Sandwich Shop. You and your classmates are invited to join us. Look at the menu and decide what you want. Work in small groups and write your food order.

Name	Order	Price
_____	_____	_____
_____	_____	_____
_____	_____	_____
_____	_____	_____
_____	_____	_____
_____	_____	_____
_____	_____	_____

Lunch Time Sandwich Shop

Sandwiches

Roast Beef	3.95
Ham	3.50
Salami	3.50
Pastrami	3.75
Turkey	3.75
Tuna Salad	3.30
Chicken Salad	3.35
Egg Salad	2.95

Beverages

Coffee	Small	.65
	Large	.75
Hot Chocolate	Small	.65
	Large	.75
Soft Drinks		.85
Juice		1.25

Phone 426-1138
Fax 426-1139

Now phone the Lunch Time Sandwich Shop and place your order.

A. Lunch Time Sandwich Shop.

B. Hello. I'd like to order lunch, please.

A. Okay.

B. I'd like _____.

A. Okay. Let me repeat that. You want _____.

B. That's right.

A. What's the name?

B. _____.

A. And the phone number?

B. _____.

A. That'll be ready in ____ minutes.

B. Thank you.

CULTURAL VIEWFINDER

Compare what working people do for lunch in different countries you know. How long is their lunch break? Where do they have lunch? What do they eat?

NAVIGATOR CAREER PROFILE

Daniel Garcia, Stock Clerk

Q: What's your name?

A: Daniel Garcia.

Q: Where do you work?

A: I work at the Shop and Save Supermarket.

Q: What do you do?

A: I'm a stock clerk. I put items on the shelves.

Q: Do you talk to the customers?

A: Yes. They ask me questions. I like to help them.

WHAT DO YOU THINK?

What kinds of food does Daniel Garcia put on the shelves? Does he like his job?

YOU'RE THE STOCK CLERK!

You work at the Shop and Save Supermarket. All the customers are asking you questions. What are they asking?

Dear Navigator

Dear Navigator,

When I go to fast-food restaurants, I order a hamburger, small fries, and a medium Coke. Sometimes the person next to me gets a hamburger, large fries, and a large Coke and pays the same price. I don't understand.

Sincerely,
Out to Lunch in Las Vegas

Dear Out to Lunch in Las Vegas,

Fast-food restaurants often have combination meals. It is cheaper to order these special meals than to order each item separately. These meals often have numbers. Look for signs, or ask before you order.

Enjoy your lunch!

Sincerely,
Navigator

Dear Navigator,

I don't understand something about supermarkets in this country. Why is everything wrapped in plastic? Chicken, beef, fish — they're all in packages. I can't smell the food. How do I know it's fresh? Is the food okay?

Sincerely,
Shopper in Salt Lake City

Readers:

What's your opinion about *Shopper in Salt Lake City's* problem? Discuss this with other students. Then answer the letter.

Dear Shopper in Salt Lake City,

_____

_____

_____

_____

_____

Sincerely,

_____

Now write your own
Dear Navigator letter.

Give an opinion or ask a question about food shopping in this country. Exchange letters with a classmate, and write answers to each other's letters. Then share with the class.

STAY IN SHAPE WITH THE
Supermarket **WORKOUT**

1 Get a shopping cart.

2 Walk into the supermarket.

3 Walk through the aisles.

4 Put the items you need in the cart.

6 Put the items on the checkout counter.

5 Go to a checkout line.

7 Watch the cashier scan each item.

8 Check the prices on the cash register.

BATH TISSUE
3.99

9 Put your bags in the shopping cart.

10 Pay the cashier.

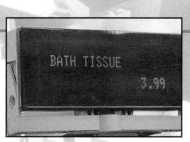

12 Check your change.

13 Walk out the door.

11 Get your change and receipt.

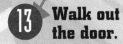

CONTRASTS
Food Shopping

- Look at the photos. What are you thinking? What are you feeling?
- What differences do you see?
- Do you see any problems? What are the solutions?
- Reflect on your own, discuss in pairs or in small groups, and share as a class.

SYNTHESIZER

Answer these questions.

COOPERATIVE TEAM
Acquiring
Organizing
Communicating
Analyzing
INFORMATION SKILLS

Do you make a shopping list before you go to buy food? _____

Where do you shop for food? _____

What's your favorite fast-food restaurant? _____

In small groups, talk about your answers to these questions. Fill in the chart for your group. Write the number of students on each line.

HOW MANY?	Your Group	Another Group	Another Group	Another Group	Another Group	Class Total
make a shopping list						
shop at						
shop at						
shop at						
shop at						
eat at						
eat at						
eat at						
eat at						

Now share as a class. Report your group's results. Fill in the other groups' results on the chart. Add up the numbers of students. Then *analyze* the information. Do many students make shopping lists? What are the favorite places to shop and eat? Why?

WordChecker

apple
beans
beef
bread
butter
cake
cheese
chicken
coffee
egg
fish
ice cream
juice
lettuce
milk
onion
orange
peach
rice
soy sauce
spice
tea
tomato
yogurt
burrito
cheeseburger
fries
hamburger
lemonade
salad
sandwich
taco

SkillChecker

I can . . .
☐ describe my food needs
☐ make a shopping list
☐ locate items in the supermarket
☐ order fast food
☐ pay for food and get change
☐ fill out a rebate coupon
☐ use the telephone to order food
☐ compare food shopping in different cultures

JOURNAL

Imagine: It's a special holiday or celebration in your family. Write about this special day.

Who is there?
What are people doing?
What are people eating?

PUZZLER PAGE

DESCRAMBLER

Unscramble these words. Then use the circled letters to make two new words and finish the sentence.

1. s i f e r   f (r) i (e) s
2. g r a m h e b u r   _ _ _ (_)(_) _ (_) _ _
3. n e c k c i h   _ _ _ _ _ (_)
4. k r n d i   _ (_) _ _ _
5. f o c e e f   _ _ _ _ _ (_)

Are you ready to order?

_ _ _ _ _ _ _ _ _, please.

EZ 4 U?

Can you read the license plate?

NEW JERSEY
I82 MUCH

Crossword

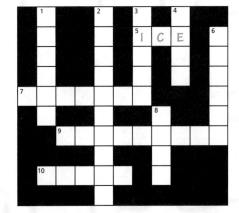

Across

5. _____ cream is my favorite dessert.
7. The _____ department has fresh fruits and vegetables.
9. A carrot is a kind of _____.
10. Milk is a _____ product.

Down

1. Bread and rolls are in the _____ section.
2. Many people buy _____ at fast-food restaurants.
3. Canned goods are in _____ three.
4. I'd like a roast _____ sandwich, please.
6. He drinks _____ every morning.
8. A _____ is a popular fast-food item from Mexico.

WORDRAP™ Checkout Line

Checkout line.
Checkout line.
Push your shopping cart
Through the checkout line.

Paper or plastic?
Cash or check?
Push your shopping cart
Through the checkout line.

Any coupons today?
Here's your receipt.
Check your change
In the checkout line.

Checkout line.
Checkout line.
Push your shopping cart
Through the checkout line.

④ At Your Service

C O N V E R S A T I O N S

50 My Apartment's on Fire!/ There's a Bad Accident!

54 You'd Better Hurry!

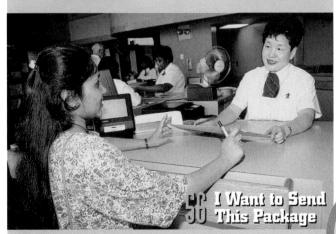

56 I Want to Send This Package

PREVIEW

Look at these three pictures.

Who do you think these people are?

What's happening?

What are they saying to each other?

52 NAVIGATOR SEARCHES THE PHONE BOOK
Emergency Telephone Numbers
Community Services

55 MAY I HELP YOU?
Navigator Goes to the Post Office

57 DID YOU HEAR?
Listening

58 LIFEWRITER
Signs and Business Hours

59 CAREER PROFILE
Louise Carter, Police Officer

60 DEAR NAVIGATOR
Your Letters on Using Community Services

61 STAY IN SHAPE
Duplicate Driver's License Workout

62 CONTRASTS
Problem-Posing Photo Essay

63 SYNTHESIZER
Cooperative Teamwork
WordChecker/SkillChecker

JOURNAL
The Community Resources You Use

64 PUZZLER PAGE
Games & Activities

WordRap™
You'd Better Hurry!

SKILLS CHECK

Can you . . .

☐ *make an emergency phone call?*

☐ *find telephone numbers in a phone book?*

☐ *read signs with business hours?*

☐ *use post office services?*

My Apartment's on Fire!

A. Emergency operator.

B. My apartment's on fire!

A. What's the address?

B. 270 Center Street, apartment 401.

A. What's your name?

B. Sara Martin.

A. Telephone number?

B. 528-4746.

A. Okay. We'll be there right away.

Practice with a partner. Report emergencies at home. Use your own personal information.

A. Emergency operator.

B. _____.

A. What's the address?

B. _____.

A. What's your name?

B. _____.

A. Telephone number?

B. _____.

A. Okay. We'll be there right away.

❶ My son is hurt.

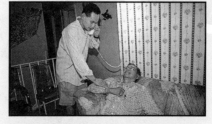

❷ My father is having a heart attack.

❸ My baby isn't breathing.

There's a Bad Accident!

A. Emergency operator.
B. There's a bad accident!
A. Where?
B. Main Street and Central Avenue.
A. What's your name?
B. Ray Sharif.
A. What phone number are you calling from?
B. 763-9421.
A. Okay. We'll be there right away.

Practice with a partner. Report emergencies in your community. Use real locations in your community.

A. Emergency operator.
B. _____.
A. Where?
B. _____.
A. What's your name?
B. _____.
A. What phone number are you calling from?
B. _____.
A. Okay. We'll be there right away.

1 There's a fire!

2 There's a big fight in our school parking lot!

3 There's a man with a gun!

NAVIGATOR SEARCHES THE PHONE BOOK

The first page of a telephone book lists emergency numbers. Here's an example of emergency numbers in one community.

FIRE 911

POLICE 911

AMBULANCE 911

Please call 911 for emergencies only.

OTHER EMERGENCY NUMBERS

Poison Control Center
562-9779

State Police
562-6611

Suicide Hotline
562-6500

U.S. Secret Service
562-6300

Now look in your phone book. Write the emergency numbers for where you live.

FIRE

POLICE

AMBULANCE

OTHER EMERGENCY NUMBERS

Poison Control Center

State Police

Suicide Hotline

U.S. Secret Service

IMPORTANT!
Call the emergency number only in a real emergency. When it isn't an emergency, call the regular telephone number.

COMMUNITY SERVICES

The telephone book has the telephone numbers of many community services. These people need information. Check the phone numbers they should call.

We're getting married in June. What are your hours?

My son needs shots for school. When are you open?

1. COURTS
   ____ Marriage License   775-1234
   ____ Traffic Violations   775-5555

2. HEALTH DEPARTMENT
   ____ Dental Clinic   979-4977
   ____ Immunizations   979-4980

I want to take the driving test.

When is registration for the next session?

3. MOTOR VEHICLES DEPARTMENT
   ____ General information   621-7000
   ____ Road test appointments   621-7550

4. PUBLIC SCHOOLS
   ____ Adult & Vocational Ed   654-9330
   ____ Personnel   654-1040

Look in your telephone book. Find the listings of services in your community. (In many phone books, these listings are on blue pages.) What services are there? What services do you need? What do you want information about? List these services and their phone numbers.

Community Service	Phone Number

You'd Better Hurry!

A. **Where are you going?**
B. **I'm going to the bank.**
A. **You'd better hurry! The bank closes at 3:00 today.**
B. **Thanks. See you.**
A. **Bye.**

Practice with a partner. Read the signs to find today's hours at these places in the community.

A. Where are you going?
B. I'm going to the _____.
A. You'd better hurry! The _____ closes at _____ today.
B. Thanks. See you.
A. Bye.

1

✚ Clinic

Mon–Fri	8:30 – 7:30
Sat	8:30 – 5:30
Sun	Closed

2

Post Office

Mon–Fri	8:00 – 5:00
Sat	8:00 – 1:00
Sun	Closed

3

Library

Hours

M, W, F	8:30 AM – 9:00 PM
T, Th	9:00 AM – 6:00 PM
Sat, Sun	11:00 AM – 7:00 PM

4

Motor Vehicles Department

Open

M–Th	8:30 – 4:30
Fri	8:30 – 7:00
Sat	9:00 – 12:00
Closed Sunday	

NAVIGATOR *goes to the post office and asks:* *May I help you?*

Yes. I want to *mail this package.*

buy ten stamps

mail this letter

buy an aerogramme

buy five postcards

send a registered letter

pick up a package

pick up my mail

send this express mail

stop my mail

Practice conversations with a partner. Use all these post office services.

A. May I help you?

B. Yes. I want to _____.

Navigator 1

55

I Want to Send This Package

A. I want to send this package to India by air mail.
B. Okay. Anything else?
A. No. That's all.
B. That's $12.76.
A. Thank you.
B. You're welcome.

Practice with a partner. Use these postal services. Decide the prices of the items and services.

A. I want to _____ .
B. Okay. Anything else?
A. No. That's all.
B. That's _____ .
A. Thank you.
B. You're welcome.

❶ mail this letter

❷ mail this package

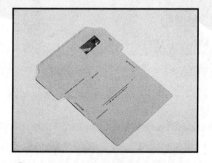

❸ buy an aerogramme

❹ buy five postcards

❺ send this letter express mail

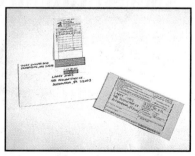

❻ send this letter certified

Did You Hear?

EMERGENCY!
Listen and circle the correct response.

1. (Ali Said)   342-1960
2. Susana Lopez   358-1071
3. 14 Oak Street   Carol Smith

5. 410-6732   207
6. River Road   Bob Wilson
7. 3121 11th Street 671-8294

WHAT'S THE SCHEDULE?
Listen to the recorded announcement. Circle the correct information.

1. (9:00 – 5:00)   10 – 5
2. 8:30 – 2:00   8:30 – 2:30
3. 8:00 – 4:30   8:00 – 4:00
4. 9:00 – 5:30   9:30 – 5:30

5. Thursday   Tuesday
6. Sunday   Monday
7. T, Th   T, F
8. M – F   M, W, F

HOW MUCH IS IT?
Listen to the conversation at the post office. Circle the amount you hear.

1. $.32   ($.72)
2. $1.10 $10.00
3. $.45 $.85
4. $2.83 $5.83

5. $1.37 $1.70
6. $.55 $.75
7. $6.50 $6.15
8. $3.23 $3.73

LIFEWRITER

SIGNS AND BUSINESS HOURS

Signs at the entrances of public buildings and stores often give business hours. Go to four places in your community. Write down the business hours on the signs. Then practice with a partner. Ask each other questions about the signs.

Library Hours

Mon, Wed, Thurs	9:00 — 9:00
Fri	9:00 — 5:00
Sat	11:00 — 6:00
Closed Tues, Sun, and Holidays	

What time does the library open on Wednesday?
When does it close on Friday?
When is the library open on the weekend?
What are the hours of the library today?

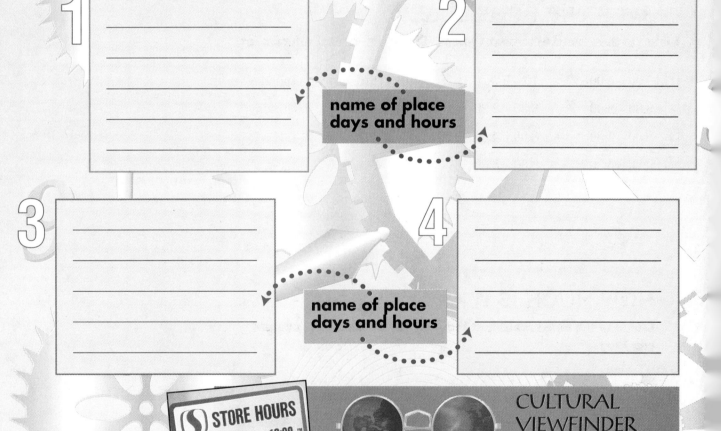

1
_____
_____
_____
_____
_____

2
_____
_____
_____
_____
_____

name of place
days and hours

3
_____
_____
_____
_____
_____

4
_____
_____
_____
_____
_____

name of place
days and hours

STORE HOURS

DAILY	6:00 AM	– 12:00	PM
SATURDAY	6:00 AM	– 12:00	PM
SUNDAY	8:00 AM	– 9:00	PM

CULTURAL VIEWFINDER

Compare business hours in different countries you know. What are the days and hours of different places?

NAVIGATOR CAREER PROFILE

Tywanna Wright, Police Officer

Q: What do you do on your job?

A: I protect the community. I make sure people obey the laws, I respond to emergencies, and I talk to people about safety.

Q: Do you drive a police car?

A: Some days I drive a police cruiser. Other days I patrol on foot downtown.

Q: Is it a dangerous job?

A: Sometimes, but it's important to keep the community safe.

Q: How does your family feel about your job?

A: They're proud of me, and they're happy when I come home at night.

WHAT DO YOU THINK?

What laws must people obey?

Why is a police officer's job sometimes dangerous?

Why is Officer Wright's family happy when she comes home at night?

SAFETY TIPS

Here are some safety tips Officer Wright gives the people in her community.

- Never open the door for strangers.
- Don't carry a lot of money in your wallet.
- Don't walk alone on a dark street.
- Call the police when you see a problem.

Work with a partner or small group. Write more safety tips.

Dear Navigator

Dear Navigator,

My daughter was sick last week. We don't have a doctor, so I took her to the emergency room at the hospital. They helped my daughter, but they were very angry. They said it wasn't an emergency. But what should we do? We don't have money for a doctor.

Sincerely,

Parent in San Francisco

Dear Parent in San Francisco,

Look for a public health clinic in your community. These clinics have nurses and doctors. They do medical examinations. Some clinics cost a little money, and some are free. In a real emergency, go to the emergency room. But for small medical problems, use the clinic.

Sincerely,

Navigator

Dear Navigator,

I'm very concerned about crime in my apartment building. Somebody broke into our apartment last month. Yesterday in the elevator a group of boys took money from my children. Two men stand in front of our building every night and sell drugs. My friend says to call the police. But back home in my country, the police did bad things to people. What should I do?

Sincerely,

Worried Immigrant in Chicago

Readers: What's your opinion about *Worried Immigrant in Chicago's* problem? Discuss this with other students. Then answer the letter.

Dear Worried Immigrant in Chicago,

_____

_____

_____

_____

_____

Sincerely,

_____

Now write your own
Dear Navigator letter.

Ask a question about services in your community. Exchange letters with a classmate, and write answers to each other's letters. Then share with the class.

Duplicate Driver's License WORKOUT

1 Oh, no! You lost your driver's license! You need a new one.

2 Go to the Motor Vehicles Department.

3 Ask for a Duplicate License form.

4 Fill out the form.

5 Get in line.

6 Give the form to the clerk.

7 Show the clerk some identification.

8 Get in another line.

9 Pay the cashier.

10 Sit down and wait. Listen for your name.

11 Go to the photographer.

13 Sit down and wait again.

12 Look into the camera and smile!

14 Get your new license.

CONTRASTS

*Putting Their Money
in a Safe Place*

Look at the photos. What are you thinking? What are you feeling?
What are the situations? What differences do you see?
Do you see any problems? What are the solutions?
Reflect on your own, discuss in pairs or in small groups, and share as a class.

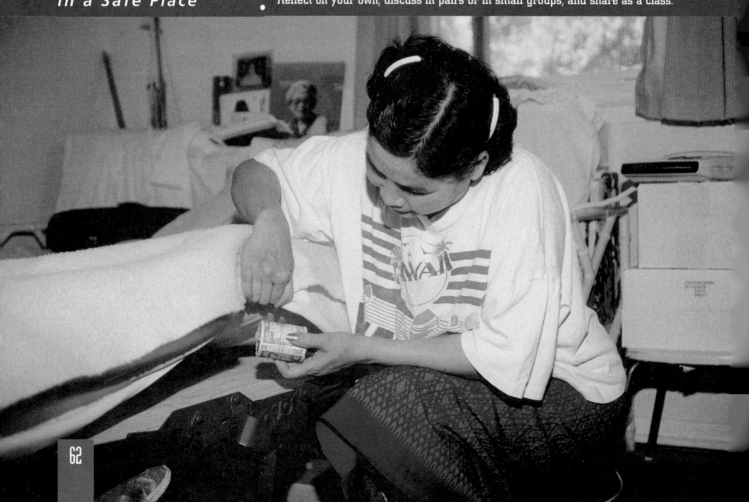

SYNTHESIZER

Check the community resources you use.

- [ ] the bank
- [ ] the post office
- [ ] the clinic
- [ ] the library

List other community resources you use.

_____   _____

In small groups, talk about community resources. Fill in the chart for your group. Write the number of students on each line.

HOW MANY?	Your Group	Another Group	Another Group	Another Group	Another Group	Class Total
use the bank						
use the post office						
use the clinic						
use the library						

Now share as a class. Report your group's resuts. Fill in the other groups' results on the chart. Add up the numbers of students. Then *analyze* the information. What community services do most students use? Why? What services don't students use? Why not?

WordChecker

accident
ambulance
emergency
 operator
fight
fire
gun
heart attack
hurt
bank
clinic
court
health
 department
library

motor vehicles
 department
post office
public school
aerogramme
certified
express mail
letter
mail
package
post card
registered
 letter
stamp

SkillChecker

I can . . .
- [ ] make emergency phone calls
- [ ] find emergency numbers in a phone book
- [ ] find telephone numbers of community services in a phone book
- [ ] read signs with business hours
- [ ] use post office services

JOURNAL

Write about the community resources you use.

Where do you go?
When are these places open?
What do you do in these places?
How do you feel there?
Do you have any problems at these places? Describe them.

PUZZLER PAGE

WordSearcher
Can you find the words?

Y	G	C	C	L	O	S	E	P	S
P	G	M	Y	V	V	N	M	Z	T
A	P	F	I	R	E	K	E	F	A
C	Y	Z	S	O	F	L	R	Y	M
K	J	O	H	J	B	A	G	D	P
A	G	L	P	M	D	A	E	N	A
G	H	J	P	E	K	F	N	D	U
E	P	X	E	S	N	K	C	K	R
F	L	I	B	R	A	R	Y	T	Q
H	J	W	T	U	G	F	J	R	I

BANK	FIRE	PACKAGE
CLOSE	LIBRARY	STAMP
EMERGENCY	OPEN	

What's the object?
Who uses it?
When? Where?

EZ 4 U?
Can you read the license plates?

ILLINOIS
FR FITR

MICHIGAN
PO WKR

TEXAS
IMA DR

Special Delivery

Can you match the states with their postal abbreviations?

Maine	MS
Maryland	MI
Massachusetts	MN
Michigan	MT
Minnesota	ME
Mississippi	MA
Missouri	MO
Montana	MD

WORDRAP™

You'd Better Hurry!

A. Where are you going?
B. To the clinic.
A. You'd better hurry! It closes at one.
B. Are you sure?
A. Yes, I'm sure. I'm absolutely sure.
The clinic closes at one.

A. Where are you going?
B. To the library.
A. You'd better hurry. It closes at two.
B. Are you sure?
A. Yes, I'm sure. I'm absolutely sure.
The library closes at two.

Now write your own raps. Use other community resources and times.

5 Your Home

CONVERSATIONS

66 I'm Looking for an Apartment

68 I'd Like to Buy a Money Order

69 There's Something Wrong with My Oven

PREVIEW

Look at these three pictures.

Who do you think these people are?

What's happening?

What are they saying to each other?

SKILLS CHECK

Can you . . .

☐ *rent an apartment?*
☐ *describe your home?*
☐ *read bills?*
☐ *buy and fill out a money order?*
☐ *request apartment repairs?*
☐ *fill out a rental application form?*
☐ *read a floor plan?*

I'm Looking for an Apartment

A. Can I help you?

B. Yes. I'm looking for an apartment.

A. How many bedrooms?

B. One.

A. We have a one-bedroom apartment available.

B. Great. How much is the rent?

A. It's $450.

B. Does that include utilities?

A. Yes, it does. Do you want to see it?

B. Yes. Please.

Practice with a partner. Look for apartments. Talk about the number of bedrooms and the rent.

A. Can I help you?

B. Yes. I'm looking for an apartment.

A. How many bedrooms?

B. _____.

A. We have a _____ available.

B. Great. How much is the rent?

A. It's _____.

B. Does that include utilities?

A. Yes, it does. Do you want to see it?

B. Yes. Please.

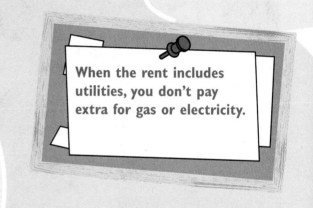

When the rent includes utilities, you don't pay extra for gas or electricity.

WHAT DO YOU THINK?

What are some good ways to look for a place to live in your area? Brainstorm with a partner. Then share your ideas as a class.

CULTURAL VIEWFINDER

Compare the types housing in different countries you know. How are the types housing different in urban and rural are

NAVIGATOR asks:

What do you like about your home?

It has *a dining room.*

a big living room

two bathrooms

three bedrooms

a parking lot

carpeting

a yard

a balcony

many windows

air conditioning

Practice conversations with a partner.

A. What do you like about your home?

B. It has _____.

PERSON TO PERSON

Talk with a partner. Ask questions about your partner's apartment or house. Then tell the class about your partner's home.

A. Does your home have _____?

B. Yes, it does./No, it doesn't.

A. Does it have _____?

B. Yes, it does./No, it doesn't.

Navigator 1

I'd Like to Buy a Money Order

A. I'd like to buy a money order for $550.
B. Did you say $515 or $550?
A. $550. Five-five-zero.
B. All right. That'll be $551.
A. Okay.

⬛R Reed Apartments

Account #R-251

PAST DUE	.00
MAY RENT	550.00
AMOUNT DUE NOW	**550.00**

Practice with a partner. Buy money orders to pay these rents.

Kenmore Towers

Account #762G

Past Due	.00
Aug Rent	370.00
Amount Due Now	**370.00**

1. $317 or $370?

A. I'd like to buy a money order for $_____.
B. Did you say $_____ or $_____?
A. $_____. _____-_____-_____.
B. All right. That'll be $_____.
A. Okay.

Martin Apartments

Unit # 114

Past Due	408.00
Dec Rent	408.00
Amount Due Now	816.00

2. $816 or $860?

You can buy money orders at post offices, supermarkets, banks, convenience stores, and check-cashing businesses. Money orders usually cost less at the post office.

WHAT DO YOU THINK?

What are different ways people pay rent?

Why are money orders important for many people?

There's Something Wrong with My Oven

A. Hello. Reed Apartments.

B. Hello. This is Sarah Kaye in apartment 251. There's something wrong with my oven.

A. Your oven? Okay. We'll send someone over to check it.

B. Thank you.

Practice with a partner. Call about apartment problems.

A. Hello. Reed Apartments.

B. Hello. This is _____ in _____.
There's something wrong with my _____.

A. Your _____? Okay. We'll send someone over to check it.

B. Thank you.

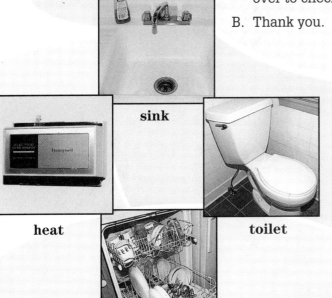

sink

heat

toilet

dishwasher

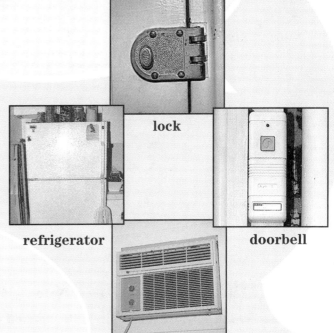

lock

refrigerator

doorbell

air conditioner

TALK ABOUT IT

What are common problems in apartments and houses? Who takes care of these problems? Brainstorm with a partner. Then share your ideas as a class.

Did You Hear?

THERE'S SOMETHING WRONG WITH MY OVEN
Listen to the conversation. Check the correct picture.

 1 ___
 ✓

 2 ___
 ___

 3 ___
 ___

 4 ___
 ___

 5 ___
 ___

 6 ___
 ___

I'D LIKE TO BUY A MONEY ORDER
Listen to the conversation. Circle the amount you hear.

1	$515	($550)		5	$518	$580
2	$313	$330		6	$614	$640
3	$716	$760		7	$219	$290
4	$417	$470		8	$415	$450

LIFEWRITER

A RENTAL APPLICATION

You want to rent an apartment. Can you fill out this rental application?

R Reed Apartments

Name _____ Date of Application _____

Telephone No. _____ Social Security No. _____

Present Address:

_____

Number   Street

                                                                    Apt.

_____

City   State   Zip Code

How long at present address? _____

Previous Address:

_____

Number   Street

                                                                    Apt.

_____

City   State   Zip Code

How long at previous address? _____

Name of each occupant   Age   Sex   Relationship

_____   ___   ___   _____

_____   ___   ___   _____

_____   ___   ___   _____

_____   ___   ___   _____

Signature of applicant _____

FLOOR PLANS

Rental offices in some big apartment buildings have floor plans. Compare the floor plans for these two apartments. Then fill in the chart.

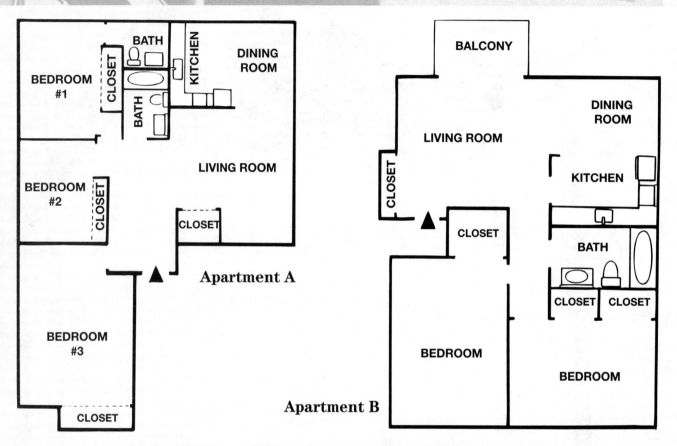

	Apartment A	Apartment B
Number of bedrooms		
Number of bathrooms		
Number of closets		
Balcony	☐ Yes ☐ No	☐ Yes ☐ No

Now talk about the floor plans in pairs or in small groups. Then share as a class.

How many people can live in Apartment A? in Apartment B? How much is the rent for Apartment A? for Apartment B? Which apartment do you want to rent? Why?

Apartment buildings have rules about the number of people in an apartment. What are the rules in buildings in your area? Are these rules a problem for some people? Why?

PAYING BILLS

Most people pay bills by check or money order. On each bill circle the amount you
have to pay. Then match the bills with the money orders.

__d__ 1

Village Apts.

Past Due	.00
Sept. rent	475.00
Amount due	**475.00**

---

a

UNITED EXPRESS MONEY ORDER

Pay
****$24.88
Exactly

****Twenty-four Dollars and 88/100ths****

PAY TO THE
ORDER OF _____

ISSUED BY _____

____ 2

 All Power Company

Last payment $25.76

For service from 2/15/98 to
3/14/98

Current charge $24.88

---

b

UNITED EXPRESS MONEY ORDER

Pay
****$25.65
Exactly

****Twenty-five Dollars and 65/100ths****

PAY TO THE
ORDER OF _____

ISSUED BY _____

____ 3

Metro
Cable TV

Basic service	$19.65
Premium One	6.00
Due by 7/1/98	**$25.65**

---

c

UNITED EXPRESS MONEY ORDER

Pay
****$22.39
Exactly

****Twenty-two Dollars and 39/100ths****

PAY TO THE
ORDER OF _____

ISSUED BY _____

____ 4

Colonial Gas Co.

Service Dates:
1/1/98 to 1/31/98

Current charges	$17.39
Balance 12/31/97	5.00
Due by 2/10/98	$22.39

---

d

UNITED EXPRESS MONEY ORDER

Pay
***$475.00
Exactly

Four Hundred Seventy-five Dollars and 00/100ths

PAY TO THE
ORDER OF _____

ISSUED BY _____

A UTILITY BILL

Bills have a lot of information.
Look at this bill. What kind of utility bill is it?
What's the amount due? When?
What's the account number?

Customer Bill

NOV 15 98 Bill for:
EDUARDO VEGA

Please Pay
$ 39.09
by   Dec 10

Meter Readings		Kilowatt Hour Usage	Summary of Charges	
			Description	Amount
NOV 14 98	OCT 12 98	363	Residential - Schedule 1	36.69
63347	62984		Utility Tax	2.40
			Account Balance	39.09

Thank you for your last payment of $37.92 on NOV 15 98.

Important Customer Information
- Your account number is 42 47 6074 5. If you have questions, please phone your Account Representative between 7:00 A.M. and 7:00 P.M. Monday-Friday at **(703) 934-9670**. Best time to call is before 5:00 P.M. Tuesday-Friday.
- If payment in full is received by DEC 10 98, you will avoid a late payment charge of 1.5%.
- Your average daily cost is $1.11 for this 33 day billing period.

CITY POWER   2424760745

18831 C

Now pay the bill. Use this money order.

UNITED EXPRESS MONEY ORDER

45-033990559

U   C   E   11/30/98   1784
United Cash Express   630/1 0959B

45-033990559

Pay
*****$39.09
Exactly

NOT VALID OVER ONE THOUSAND DOLLARS

**********Thirty-Nine Dollars and 09/100ths**********

PAY TO THE
ORDER OF _____

ISSUED BY _____

Hilaida Rivera, Rental Manager

Q: Can you tell us something about your job?

A: Sure. I greet people. I describe for them the apartments in our building. I show them vacant apartments.

Q: What kinds of apartments do you have?

A: Most of our apartments have one bedroom or two bedrooms. We have a few three-bedroom apartments.

Q: How many people can live in an apartment?

A: It depends. Sometimes we have problems because there are too many people in one apartment. Then some people have to leave.

Q: Do you like your job?

A: Oh, yes! I like to meet new people. I like to help people. This is a nice apartment complex. We have playgrounds and a swimming pool. I'm happy when people decide to live here.

YOU'RE THE RENTAL MANAGER!

You're very busy today. Many people want to rent apartments. What are they asking?

? **Why do a lot of people sometimes live in one apartment? Why is this a problem?**

Dear Navigator

Dear Navigator,

I have a bad problem. I'm a clean person, but there are many cockroaches in my apartment. They're in the kitchen, the bathroom, and sometimes in the bedroom. It's terrible! Please help me.

Sincerely,

Going Buggy in Boston

Dear Going Buggy in Boston,

Here are some tips for your problem with cockroaches:

- Keep food in covered containers.
- Use a trash container with a lid or cover.
- Don't store bags from the supermarket.
- Buy roach bait or roach traps. (Or put boric acid where you see roaches.)

You can also ask your landlord to spray your apartment.

Good luck!

Sincerely,

Navigator

Readers: What's your opinion about *Apartment Hunter in Huntington Beach's* problem? Discuss this with other students. Then answer the letter.

Dear Apartment Hunter in Huntington Beach,

_____

_____

_____

_____

_____

Sincerely,

_____

Dear Navigator,

My three brothers, two sisters, and I want to rent one apartment and live together. Nobody will rent to us. They say we are too many people. We don't understand. We're a family. We lived together in our country. We want to stay together here, too. And apartment rents are so expensive. We want to share the rent. Why can't we live together?

Sincerely,

Apartment Hunter in Huntington Beach

Now write your own
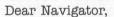 **letter.**

Describe a problem about your apartment or house, or ask a question about housing. Exchange letters with a classmate, and write answers to each other's letters. Then share with the class.

Leaky Faucet WORKOUT

1 Go to the sink.

2 Turn on the hot water.

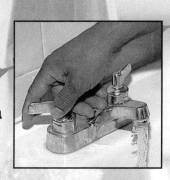

3 Turn on the cold water.

Wash your hands. **4**

6 Turn off the cold water.

5 Turn off the hot water.

7 Watch the water. It's dripping.

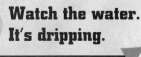

8 Tighten the handles.

9 The water is still dripping!

Dry your hands. **10**

Go to the phone. **11**

12 Call the landlord and report the problem.

CONTRASTS
Home

- Look at the photos. What are you thinking? What are you feeling?
- What differences do you see?
- Do you see any problems? What are the solutions?
- Reflect on your own, discuss in pairs or in small groups, and share as a class.

SYNTHESIZER

Check the sentences that are true for you.

- [ ] I rent.
- [ ] I own.
- [ ] I repair things in my home.
- [ ] I call the landlord to repair things in my home.

- [ ] I pay for utilities.
- [ ] I pay bills with cash.
- [ ] I pay bills with checks.
- [ ] I pay bills with money orders.

In small groups, talk about students' answers. Fill in the chart for your group. Write the number of students on each line.

HOW MANY STUDENTS	Your Group	Another Group	Another Group	Another Group	Another Group	Class Total
rent?						
own?						
repair things?						
call the landlord?						
pay for utilities?						
pay bills with cash?						
pay bills with checks?						
pay bills with money orders?						

Now share as a class. Report your group's results. Fill in the other groups' results on the chart. Add up the numbers of students. Then *analyze* the information. How many students repair things at home? What bills do students pay? How do they pay them?

WordChecker

air conditioner
air conditioning
apartment
available
balcony
bathroom
bedroom
carpeting
dining room
dishwasher
floor plan
heat
living room
lock
oven

parking lot
refrigerator
rent
sink
toilet
utilities
window
yard

amount due
bill
check
money order

SkillChecker

I can . . .
- [ ] ask about an apartment for rent
- [ ] describe my home
- [ ] read bills
- [ ] buy a money order
- [ ] fill out a money order
- [ ] request apartment repairs
- [ ] fill out a rental application form
- [ ] read a floor plan

JOURNAL

Write about your home.

Do you live in a house or an apartment?
What rooms does it have?
Describe all the rooms.
What do you like about your home?
What problems are there in your home?

PUZZLER PAGE

DESCRAMBLER

Unscramble these words about housing. Then use the circled letters to make a new word and finish the sentence.

1. t r e n — r (e) n t
2. a t n o u m — _ (O)(O) _ _ (O)
3. l i b l — (O) _ _ _
4. h e p o n — _ (O)(O) _ (O)
5. r e d r o — _ (O)(O)(O) _

We're looking for a

_ _ _ _ _ _   _ _ _ _ _ _ _ _ _

apartment.

CLOSE-UP

What's the object? Where is it in a home? How do you use it?

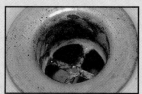

WORDRAP™

I Hate My Old Apartment!

I hate my old apartment!
My very old apartment!
The rooms are small.
There aren't many closets.
The ceilings are low.
And the rent is high.
The neighbors are noisy.
The landlord is nasty.
The windows face a
  brick wall.
It's a terrible view.
I hate my old apartment!
I really want to move!

I Love My New Apartment!

I love my new apartment!
My very new apartment!
The rooms are large.
There are lots and lots
  of closets.
The ceilings are high.
And the rent is low.
The neighbors are quiet.
The landlord is friendly.
The windows face
  the beach.
It's a wonderful view.
I love my new apartment!
I never want to move!

Crossword

							1	
2 U	T	I	L	I	T	I	E	S
			3					
	4							
					5			
	6						7	
8								
9								

Across

2. Gas and electricity are called ____.
4. The amount ____ is how much you have to pay.
6. You take a shower in the ____.
9. You cook in the ____.

Down

1. You sleep in the ____.
3. People pay ____ every month.
5. "There's something ____" means there's a problem.
7. You bake cakes in an ____.
8. There's a ____ in the kitchen and in the bathroom.

6 Taking Care of Yourself

CONVERSATIONS

82 I Have a Headache

84 I'd Like to Make an Appointment

85 Take One Tablet Four Times a Day

PREVIEW

Look at these three pictures.

Who do you think these people are?

What's happening?

What are they saying to each other?

SKILLS CHECK

Can you . . .
- [ ] *talk about health problems?*
- [ ] *talk about injuries?*
- [ ] *make a doctor's appointment?*
- [ ] *understand prescription drug labels?*
- [ ] *fill out a medical history form?*

I Have a Headache

A. Is anything wrong?
B. Yes. I don't feel well.
A. What's the matter?
B. I have a headache.
A. Oh. I'm sorry to hear that.

Practice with a partner. Talk about what's wrong.

A. Is anything wrong?
B. Yes. I don't feel well.
A. What's the matter?
B. I have a _____.
A. Oh. I'm sorry to hear that.

1 stomachache

2 backache

3 toothache

4 sore throat

5 cold

6 cough

THINK ABOUT IT
What are some other medical problems people have?

What's the matter?

I hurt my *hand*.

head

leg

elbow

ankle

back

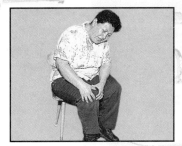

knee

wrist

toe

arm

foot

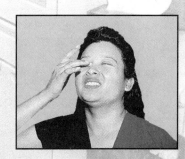

eye

neck

Practice conversations with a partner.

A. What's the matter?

B. I hurt my _____.

I'd Like to Make an Appointment

A. Hello. Doctor's office.

B. Hello. This is Domingo Fernandez. I'd like to make an appointment with the doctor.

A. What's the problem?

B. I have a bad cough.

A. I see. Can you come in tomorrow at 10:00?

B. Tomorrow at 10:00? Yes, that's fine. Thank you.

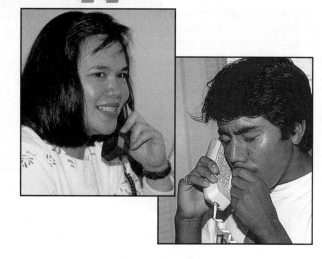

Practice with a partner. Describe health problems and injuries. Make a doctor's appointment.

A. Hello. Doctor's office.

B. Hello. This is _____. I'd like to make an appointment with the doctor.

A. What's the problem?

B. _____.

A. I see. Can you come in _____?

B. _____? Yes, that's fine. Thank you.

1 **I have a stomachache.**
today at 4:15

2 **I hurt my back.**
Wednesday at 10:30

3 **I hurt my foot.**
tomorrow at 11:45

4 **I have a bad toothache.**
Friday at 2:00

5 **I have a bad sore throat.**
Tuesday at 3:15

6 **I hurt my arm.**
Thursday at 1:30

THINK ABOUT IT
When should you see a doctor?

Take One Tablet Four Times a Day

A. Can you tell me how to take this, please?
B. Sure. Take one tablet four times a day.
A. One tablet four times a day?
B. That's right.
A. Thank you.

KING'S PHARMACY

one tablet four times a day

℞

Practice with a partner. Explain the directions on medicine labels.

A. Can you tell me how to take this, please?
B. Sure. Take _____.
A. _____?
B. That's right.
A. Thank you.

Main St. Pharmacy ℞

one teaspoon two times a day

1.

County ℞

one capsule before meals

2.

S&B

℞ one tablet every four hours

3.

Delta Drugs

two pills as needed for pain

4.

Olympic Pharmacies

one tablet every six hours

5.

Mountain Pharmacy

℞ two teaspoons after meals

6.

Did You Hear?

CAN YOU COME ON THURSDAY AT 3:00?

Listen to the conversations between patients and receptionists. Circle the correct appointment time.

1	(Thursday at 3:00)	Monday at 3:00	4	Friday at 1:00	Friday at 4:00
2	Wednesday at 12:15	Friday at 12:15	5	Thursday at 2:00	Thursday at 2:30
3	Tuesday at 10:30	Thursday at 10:30	6	Tuesday at 11:45	Tuesday at 11:15

TAKE TWO TABLETS THREE TIMES A DAY

Listen to each conversation between a customer and a pharmacist. Check the correct label.

1

KING'S PHARMACY		KING'S PHARMACY	
one tablet with meals R_x	✓	two tablets with meals R_x	____

2

Main St. Pharmacy R_x		Main St. Pharmacy R_x	
two teaspoons every four hours	____	three teaspoons every four hours	____

3

County R_x		County R_x	
two pills every two hours	____	two pills every three hours	____

4

S&B R_x		S&B R_x	
one capsule as needed	____	two capsules as needed	____

5

Delta Drugs		Delta Drugs	
one teaspoon three times a day	____	one teaspoon every three hours	____

LifeWRITER

MEDICAL HISTORY

Name _____
       Last   First   M.I.

Address _____
        Number   Street   Apt. #

_____
       City   State   Zip Code

Telephone: Home _____ Work _____

Social Security Number _____ Date of Birth _____

Emergency Contact: Name _____ Telephone _____

Person Responsible for Paying Bill _____ Relationship _____

Please answer the following questions:

Do you have:

headaches?   Yes ☐   No ☐

trouble sleeping? Yes ☐   No ☐

trouble eating?   Yes ☐   No ☐

Other problem (specify)   Yes ☐   No ☐

_____

Did you ever have surgery?   Yes ☐   No ☐

Are you taking any medicine now? Yes ☐   No ☐

Signature _____

                             Date _____

MEDICINE LABELS

HOW MUCH MEDICINE?
Match the medicine label with the correct picture.

KING'S PHARMACY

2 capsules every 4 hours

Rx

_d_ **1.**

Main St. Pharmacy Rx

1 tablet every 3 hours

___ **2.**

County Rx

2 teaspoons 2 times a day

___ **3.**

S&B

Rx   1 teaspoon
3 times a day

___ **4.**

a

b

c

d

THE CORRECT DOSAGE

Read the medicine label and draw a line on the medicine cup to mark the correct dosage.

Delta Drugs

take 1 teaspoon
every 6 hours

READ LABEL
— 3 TSP —
— 2 TSP —
— 1 TSP —

Olympic Pharmacies

Take 2 teaspoons every
4 hours as needed for cough

READ LABEL
— 3 TSP —
— 2 TSP —
— 1 TSP —

Mountain Pharmacy

Rx   Take 1 1/2 teaspoons
3 times a day until
finished

READ LABEL
— 3 TSP —
— 2 TSP —
— 1 TSP —

Drug stores and supermarkets
sell special cups and spoons
for measuring medicine.

tsp. = teaspoon
3 tsp. = 1 Tablespoon

CULTURAL VIEWFINDER

**Compare medicine in
different countries you
know. What kinds of medicine do people take
for different problems? Where do people get
their medicine?**

Grace Paulino, Medical Technician

Q: Where do you work?

A: I work at a public health clinic.

Q: Do all medical technicians work at clinics?

A: No. Medical technicians also work at hospitals, doctor's offices, nursing homes, and laboratories.

Q: What do you do at the clinic?

A: I draw blood and take throat cultures. Sometimes I do simple lab tests.

Q: Are you worried about diseases?

A: Not really. I'm very careful.

Q: Do you like your job?

A: Yes, but I studied medicine in my country. One day, I want to be a doctor.

WHAT DO YOU THINK?

Who goes to public health clinics?

Why is Grace always careful?

Will it be easy for her to become a doctor?

Do you have plans for a different job? What are they?

CHECK IT OUT

Bring this information to class and share it with your classmates.

Where is the nearest public health clinic in your area?
What services does it provide?
What are the costs?
When is it open?

Dear Navigator

Dear Navigator,

My daughter will go to school for the first time in September. Today I got a letter from the school. It said she needs immunizations. Medicine is so expensive in the United States. I don't have medical insurance. How can I pay for this?

Sincerely,

Kindergarten Mom in Kansas City

Dear Kindergarten Mom in Kansas City,

Is there a public health clinic in your community? These clinics give immunizations free of charge or at low cost. Call the school. Someone there will tell you where to go.

Sincerely,

Navigator

Dear Navigator,

I don't have a doctor. I don't have much money. I <u>do</u> have a very bad cough. In my native country things were different. My neighbor gave me shots of penicillin when I was sick. Here, I can't buy penicillin shots in the stores. Why not? What should I do about my cough?

Sincerely,

Hacking Away in Hackensack

Readers: What's your opinion about *Hacking Away in Hackensack's* problem? Discuss this with other students. Then answer the letter.

Dear Hacking Away in Hackensack,

_____

_____

_____

_____

_____

Sincerely,

_____

Now write your own

Dear Navigator letter.

Give an opinion or ask a question about health care in this country. Exchange letters with a classmate, and write answers to each other's letters. Then share with the class.

Medical Checkup WORKOUT

1 Take off your shoes.

2 Step on the scale.

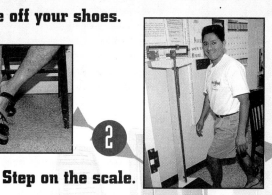

3 Check your weight.

4 Step off the scale.

Take your temperature.

7

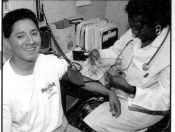

Check your blood pressure.

6

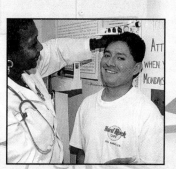

5 Measure your height.

8 Sit on the examining table.

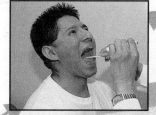

9 Open your mouth and say "Aaaahhhh."

10 Take a deep breath and hold it.

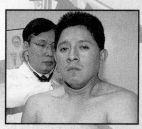

11 Exhale.

Check your reflexes.

13

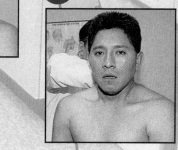

12 Listen to your heart.

14 You're in excellent shape!

CONTRASTS
Medicine

- Look at the photos. What are you thinking? What are you feeling?
- What are the situations? What differences do you see?
- Do you see any problems? What are the solutions?
- Reflect on your own, discuss in pairs or in small groups, and share as a class.

SYNTHESIZER

Check *Yes* or *No*.

Yes	No	
☐	☐	I had a checkup during the past year.
☐	☐	I was sick during the past year.
☐	☐	I have a doctor.
☐	☐	I take medicine.

In small groups, talk about students' answers. Fill in the chart for your group. Write the number of students on each line.

HOW MANY STUDENTS	Your Group	Another Group	Another Group	Another Group	Another Group	Class Total
had a checkup during the past year?						
were sick during the past year?						
have a doctor?						
take medicine?						

Now share as a class. Report your group's results. Fill in the other groups' results on the chart. Add up the numbers of students. Then *analyze* the information about your class. How many students were sick? How many students have a doctor? Do students have problems with medical care?

WordChecker

backache	ankle
cold	arm
cough	back
headache	elbow
sore throat	eye
stomachache	foot
toothache	hand
	head
	knee
capsule	leg
pill	neck
tablet	toe
teaspoon	wrist

SkillChecker

I can . . .
- ☐ talk about health problems
- ☐ talk about injuries
- ☐ make a doctor's appointment
- ☐ understand prescription drug labels
- ☐ fill out a medical history form

JOURNAL

Write about a time you were sick.

What was the problem? What did you do about it?

PUZZLER PAGE

DESCRAMBLER

Unscramble these words about medicine. Then use the circled letters to make a new word and finish the sentence.

1. s i t e m   t (i) m (e) s
2. o p e n s t a o   _ (_) _ _ _ _ _ (_)
3. l a d i y   (_) _ (_) _ _
4. s c a l e u p   (_) _ _ _ _ _ (_)

Go to the drug store and buy this

_ _ _ _ _ _ _ _ _.

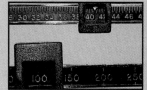

EZ 4 U?

Can you read the license plates?

NEW JERSEY
1 DCTR

MISSOURI
CAN UC

Crossword

3. F E E T

Across

3. You put your shoes on your ____.
4. Sometimes you have a sore ____ if you talk too much.
5. Your ____ is on top of your neck.
7. You have ten ____.

Down

1. You see with your ____.
2. Your ____ hurts when you eat too much.
6. You hear with your ____.

WordMaker

How many words can you make with the letters in this word?

APPOINTMENT

WORDRAP™

Oh! My Back!

A. Oh! My back!
   I just hurt my back!
B. I'm sorry to hear that.
   Is there anything I can do?
A. No. It's all right.
   My back will be okay.
B. Are you sure?
A. Yes, I'm sure. But thanks anyway.

Now write your own raps about other things that hurt.

7 Getting There

CONVERSATIONS

96 I'm Looking for a Post Office

28A 28B Westbound

98 Does This Bus Go to the Mall?

99 The Sign Says 25 Miles per Hour

PREVIEW

Look at these three pictures.

Who do you think these people are?

What's happening?

What are they saying to each other?

SKILLS CHECK

Can you . . .
- [ ] *ask the location of places?*
- [ ] *describe locations?*
- [ ] *ask where buses and trains go?*
- [ ] *read traffic signs?*
- [ ] *read schedules?*

I'm Looking for a Post Office

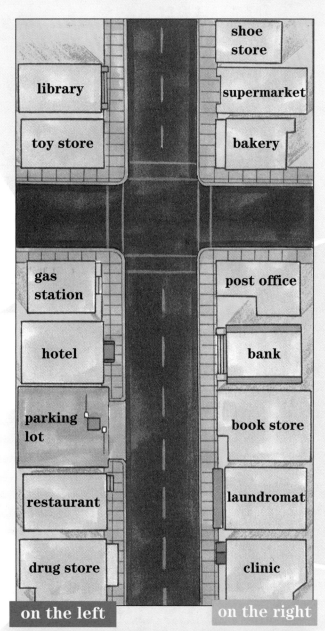

shoe store

library

supermarket

toy store

bakery

gas station

post office

hotel

bank

parking lot

book store

restaurant

laundromat

drug store

clinic

on the left

on the right

A. Excuse me. I'm looking for a post office.
B. There's a post office on the right, next to the bank.
A. On the right, next to the bank?
B. That's right.
A. Thank you.

A. Excuse me. I'm looking for a library.
B. There's a library on the left, across from the supermarket.
A. On the left, across from the supermarket?
B. That's right.
A. Thank you.

A. Excuse me. I'm looking for a laundromat.
B. There's a laundromat on the right, between the clinic and the book store.
A. On the right, between the clinic and the book store?
B. That's right.
A. Thank you.

Practice with a partner. Talk about the locations of places. Use the map on page 96.

A. Excuse me. I'm looking for a _____.

B. There's a _____ on the _____, _____.

A. On the _____, _____?

B. That's right.

A. Thank you.

1 shoe store

2 drug store

3 gas station

4 book store

5 supermarket

6 bank

7 clinic

8 parking lot

9 restaurant

10 bakery

11 hotel

12 toy store

Now practice more conversations about real locations in your community.

Does This Bus Go to the Mall?

A. Excuse me. Does this bus go the mall?
B. No, it doesn't.
A. Oh. Which bus should I take?
B. Take Bus 22A.
A. Bus 22A? Thanks.

Practice with a partner. Talk about public transportation.

A. Excuse me. Does this _____ go to _____?
B. No, it doesn't.
A. Oh. Which _____ should I take?
B. Take _____.
A. _____? Thanks.

① **train**
   14th Street
   the Number 1 train

② **bus**
   the courthouse
   the "15"

③ **train**
   Philadelphia
   the "Colonial"

④ **shuttle**
   Parking Lot C
   the blue shuttle

Now practice more conversations about real locations in your community.

THINK ABOUT IT
Who uses public transportation?
Why is public transportation important?

The Sign Says 25 Miles per Hour

A. Slow down!

B. What?

A. Slow down. The sign says 25 miles per hour.

B. Oh. I didn't see it.

Practice with a partner. Read the traffic signs and give warnings.

A. _____!

B. What?

A. _____! The sign says

_____.

B. Oh. I didn't see it.

1 **Don't turn!**

2 **Slow down!**

3 **Be careful!**

4 **Watch out!**

5 **Don't turn!**

6 **Slow down!**

Now draw more traffic signs and practice new conversations.

Did You Hear?

I'M LOOKING FOR A BANK

Listen to the conversations. Check the locations you hear.

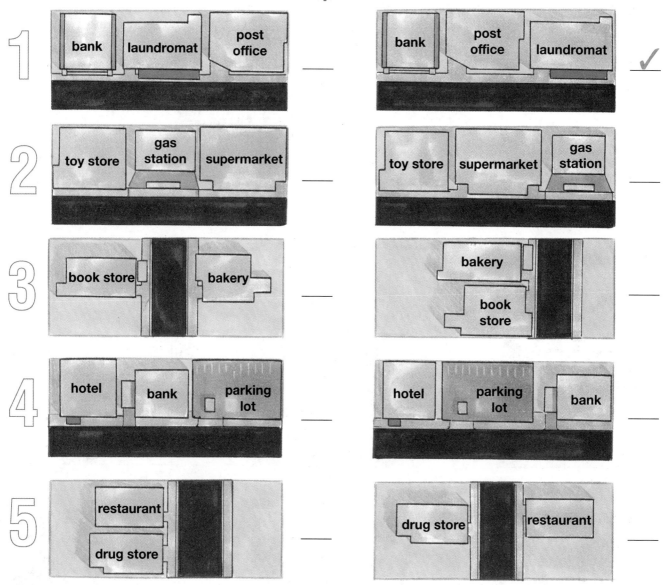

1. bank | laundromat | post office _____   bank | post office | laundromat ✓

2. toy store | gas station | supermarket _____   toy store | supermarket | gas station _____

3. book store | bakery _____   bakery | book store _____

4. hotel | bank | parking lot _____   hotel | parking lot | bank _____

5. restaurant | drug store _____   drug store | restaurant _____

FLIGHT 207 IS NOW BOARDING!

Listen to the announcements. Circle the gate number or track number you hear.

| 1 | (8) | 18 | 3 | 66 | 56 | 5 | 37 | 73 | 7 | 19 | 90 |
| 2 | 2B | 5B | 4 | 14 | 48 | 6 | 22 | 72 | 8 | 156 | 166 |

BUS SCHEDULES

Where do buses go? How often do they operate? Bus schedules give lots of information. Read this schedule. Can you answer the questions?

Route 18A

King Street	Braddock Road	Russell Avenue	Custis Drive	Metro Plaza
Weekdays				
5:40 AM	5:51	6:01	6:06	6:13
6:00	6:11	6:21	6:26	6:33
6:20	6:31	6:41	6:46	6:53
6:40	6:51	7:01	7:06	7:13
7:00	7:11	7:21	7:26	7:33
7:20	7:31	7:41	7:46	7:53
7:40	7:51	8:01	8:06	8:13
8:00	8:11	8:21	8:26	8:33
8:20	8:31	8:41	8:46	8:53
8:40	8:51	9:01	9:06	9:13
9:00	9:11	9:21	9:26	9:33
10:05	10:15	10:25	10:30	-
11:05	11:15	11:25	11:30	-
12:05 PM	12:15	12:25	12:30	-
1:05	1:15	1:25	1:30	-
2:05	2:15	2:25	2:30	-
3:05	3:16	3:26	3:31	3:38
3:50	4:01	4:11	4:16	4:23
4:10	4:21	4:31	4:36	4:43
4:30	4:41	4:51	4:56	5:03
4:50	5:01	5:11	5:16	5:23
5:10	5:21	5:31	5:36	5:43
5:30	5:41	5:51	5:56	6:03
5:50	6:01	6:11	6:16	6:23
6:10	6:21	6:31	6:36	6:43
6:30	6:41	6:51	6:56	7:03
6:50	7:01	7:11	7:16	7:23

1. Where does the bus route start?
2. Where does the bus route end?
3. What time does the first bus leave King Street?
4. What time does the first bus arrive at Metro Plaza?
5. What time does the last bus leave King Street?
6. What time does the last bus arrive at Braddock Road?
7. When does the 6:00 A.M. bus arrive at Russell Avenue?
8. When does the 4:30 P.M. bus arrive at Custis Drive?
9. Which buses do not stop at Metro Plaza?
10. How long does it take the 3:05 bus to reach Metro Plaza?

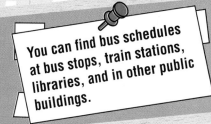

You can find bus schedules at bus stops, train stations, libraries, and in other public buildings.

Your Bus Schedules

Bring in bus schedules for your community. Discuss with your classmates: Where do the buses go? How often do they operate?

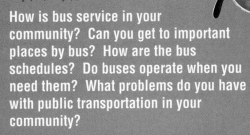

TALK ABOUT IT

How is bus service in your community? Can you get to important places by bus? How are the bus schedules? Do buses operate when you need them? What problems do you have with public transportation in your community?

CULTURAL VIEWFINDER

Compare public transportation in different countries you know. How do people get around? What are different types of transportation like? Do they operate on schedule?

What's Your Sign?

Signs are everywhere! Do you know the meanings of these signs?

a. The speed limit is 35 miles per hour.
b. You have to stop.
c. You can't turn right.
d. There's a school nearby. Watch out for children.
e. You have to slow down and stop if necessary.
f. The traffic on this street goes in one direction.
g. You can't turn around.
h. Watch out for people crossing the street.
i. There's a train track ahead. Watch out for trains.
j. You can't drive through here.
k. There's a hill.
l. You can't turn right if the light is red.

1. __j__

2. ___

3. ___

4. ___

5. ___

6. ___

7. ___

8. ___

9. ___

10. ___

11. ___

12. ___

Andres Zourzoukis, Taxi Driver

Q. What's your name?

A. Andres Zourzoukis.

Q. Do you have a lot of experience as a taxi driver?

A. Yes. I have five years experience. And in my country, I drove a van.

Q. Do you own your cab?

A. No. I rent this car from the taxi company. It's expensive.

Q. What's your job like?

A. Well, it's always interesting. I drive different people every day. I like the airport because I pick up a lot of tourists. I meet people from many different places.

Q. What do you talk about with your passengers?

A. Sports, politics, the weather . . . everything!

Q. Do you need special skills to drive a taxi?

A. You need to be a good driver. You need to know your way around the city. It's important to know how to use a map.

Q. Does anything unusual ever happen?

A. Oh, yes! One time I drove a pregnant woman to the hospital. She almost had her baby in the back seat! Another time, Sylvester Stallone was my passenger. Can you believe it? "Rocky" . . . in my taxi! It was amazing!

SPRINGFIELD YELLOW CAB

WHAT DO YOU THINK?

?

Why does Andres rent his taxi from the company?

How many days a week do you think he works?

What hours does he work?

What are good things and bad things about this occupation?

YOU'RE IN THE DRIVER'S SEAT!

You're a taxi driver! You just picked up a tourist at the airport. Answer the tourist's questions about your community.

Can you recommend a good hotel?

What should I see during my visit?

Is it safe here? Are there any dangerous neighborhoods?

Can you recommend some good restaurants?

Dear Navigator

Dear Navigator,

I take the bus to my job at a hospital. Last Monday I went to the bus stop at the usual time. Nobody was there. I waited a long time for the bus to come. It was almost empty. I was late for work.

Somebody said the bus schedule was different because it was a holiday. How often does this happen?

Sincerely,

Stranded in St. Louis

Dear Stranded in St. Louis,

Buses have different schedules for weekdays, weekends, and holidays. In many cities, buses operate on a weekend schedule during holidays. Radio stations sometimes give this information. It's important to have a bus schedule so you know the different times.

Sincerely,

Navigator

Dear Navigator,

I'm very upset. I want to get my driver's license. I passed the written test. This morning I took my road test. The examiner spoke very fast. I didn't always understand his instructions. I asked him to please speak slowly, but he didn't. I didn't pass the test.

I know I'm a good driver. I never had an accident in my country. I think I failed because of my English. Is that fair?

Sincerely,

No License in Nashville

Readers: What's your opinion about *No License in Nashville's* problem? Discuss this with other students. Then answer the letter.

Dear No License in Nashville,

_____

_____

_____

_____

Sincerely,

_____

Now write your own
Dear Navigator letter.

Give an opinion or ask a question about public transportation or driving. Exchange letters with a classmate, and write answers to each other's letters. Then share with the class.

STAY IN SHAPE WITH THE
Ride-the-Bus WORKOUT

1 Read the bus schedule.

2 Go to the bus stop.

3 Wait for the bus.

6 Get on the bus.

Check the route. Is it the right bus?

4 Get in line.

5

7 Pay the fare.

8 Walk toward the back of the bus.

9 Sit down.

10 Look out the window.

Pull the cord when you see your stop.

11

13 Get off the bus.

12 Stand up.

CONTRASTS
Going to Work

Look at the photos. What are you thinking? What are you feeling?
What are the situations? What differences do you see?
Do you see any problems? What are the solutions?
Reflect on your own, discuss in pairs or in small groups, and share as a class.

SYNTHESIZER

Check the things you usually do to get around town.

- ☐ walk
- ☐ ride a bike
- ☐ drive a car
- ☐ take a taxi
- ☐ take a bus
- ☐ take a train

In small groups, talk about how students get around town. Fill in the chart for your group. Write the number of students on each line.

HOW MANY STUDENTS	Your Group	Another Group	Another Group	Another Group	Another Group	Class Total
walk?						
ride a bike?						
drive a car?						
take a taxi?						
take a bus?						
take a train?						

Now share as a class. Report your group's results. Fill in the other groups' results on the chart. Add up the numbers of students. Then *analyze* the information about your class. How do most students get around town? Why? What are the best ways to get to different places?

WordChecker

across from
between
next to
on the left
on the right
bus route
bus schedule
arrive
leave
DO NOT ENTER
NO LEFT TURN
NO RIGHT TURN
ONE WAY
STOP
YIELD
miles per hour

bakery
bank
book store
clinic
drug store
gas station
hotel
laundromat
library
parking lot
post office
restaurant
shoe store
supermarket
toy store

SkillChecker

I can . . .

- ☐ ask the location of places
- ☐ describe locations
- ☐ ask where buses and trains go
- ☐ read traffic signs
- ☐ read schedules

JOURNAL

Write about a trip you took.

Where did you go?
How did you get there?
What was the trip like?
What did you see?

PUZZLER PAGE

DESCRAMBLER

Unscramble these words about transportation. Then use the circled letters to make a new word and finish the sentence.

1. e l d i y   y i e l (d)
2. s b u   _ (_) _
3. a r c   (_) _ _
4. f e l t   _ (_) _ _
5. h o l s c o   (_) _ (_) _ _ _
6. n a l e p   _ (_) _ _ (_)

It's a good idea to look at the bus

_ _ _ _ _ _ _ _ _ _ .

CLOSE-UP

What do you see?

EZ 4 U?

Can you read the license plate?

FLORIDA
IM SO L8

WORDRAP™

Does This Bus Go to the Mall?

A. Does this bus go to the mall?

B. Yes, it does.
This bus goes to the mall.

A&B. Get on the bus!
Get on the bus!
This bus goes to the mall.

Does This Bus Go Downtown?

A. Does this bus go downtown?

B. No, it doesn't.
This bus doesn't go downtown.

A&B. Get off the bus!
Get off the bus!
This bus doesn't go downtown!

Now write your own raps about buses, trains, and planes.

WordSearcher

Can you find the words?

A	T	L	S	X	O	U	L	Q	R
E	C	U	Q	I	V	I	Q	Q	I
F	L	R	R	X	E	L	E	F	G
Z	B	Q	O	N	E	X	T	L	H
I	E	Y	Q	S	G	O	V	Q	T
F	T	T	N	I	S	L	Y	Z	J
L	W	M	G	Q	T	S	B	Z	C
U	E	W	U	Y	O	Z	L	X	D
E	E	W	T	L	P	S	L	O	L
E	N	T	E	R	I	H	B	H	W

ACROSS   SLOW   NEXT
ENTER   TURN   BETWEEN
RIGHT   STOP

WordMaker

How many words can you make with the letters in this word?

TRANSPORTATION

Be a Smart Shopper

CONVERSATIONS

110 **Do You Have This Shirt in Blue?**

111 **Do You Have This Dress in a Size 10?**

113 **Excuse Me. Is This on Sale?**

PREVIEW

Look at these three pictures.

Who do you think these people are?

What's happening?

What are they saying to each other?

SKILLS CHECK

Can you . . .

- [ ] *shop for clothing?*
- [ ] *ask about color?*
- [ ] *ask about size?*
- [ ] *ask about price?*
- [ ] *talk about fit?*
- [ ] *read price tags?*
- [ ] *read store sale ads?*
- [ ] *write checks?*

Do You Have This Shirt in Blue?

A. Excuse me.
B. Yes? Can I help you?
A. Do you have this shirt in blue?
B. Let me check.

A. Excuse me.
B. Yes? Can I help you?
A. Do you have these pants in brown?
B. Let me check.

Practice with a partner. Tell the item you're looking for.

A. Excuse me.
B. Yes. Can I help you?
A. Do you have this/these _____ in _____?
B. Let me check.

1 **sweater**
black

2 **shirt**
red

3 **blouse**
purple

4 **skirt**
green

5 **socks**
blue

6 **pants**
black

7 **shoes**
brown

8 **gloves**
black

9 **coat**
red

10 **pajamas**
blue

11 **dress**
yellow

12 **jeans**
gray

13 **sneakers**
white

14 **boots**
black

15 **hat**
gray

16 **tie**
brown

Do You Have This Dress in a Size 10?

A. Excuse me.
B. Yes? Can I help you?
A. Do you have this dress in a size 10?
B. Let me check.

A. Excuse me.
B. Yes? Can I help you?
A. Do you have this/these _____ in _____?
B. Let me check.

Practice with a partner. Tell the size you're looking for.

❶ a size 11

❷ a small

❸ a medium

❹ a 16 1/2

❺ an extra-large

❻ a size 12

❼ a size 38

❽ a size 8

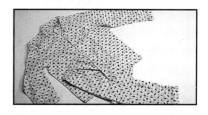
❾ a large

LOOKING FOR LABELS

Where are the labels on different kinds of clothing? What information is on the labels?

NAVIGATOR goes into the fitting room and asks:

How does it fit?/How do they fit?

It's too big.

They're too small.

It's too tight.

They're too long.

It's too short.

They're too large.

It's too loose.

Stores usually limit the number of items you can take into a fitting room.

Excuse Me. Is This on Sale?

A. Excuse me. Is this on sale?
B. Yes. It's on sale for $15.00.
A. Great. I'll take it.
B. Cash, check, or charge?
A. Check.

Practice with a partner. Find out the sale price.

A. Excuse me. Is this on sale?
B. Yes. It's on sale for _____.
A. Great. I'll take it.
B. Cash, check, or charge?
A. Check.

A. Excuse me. Are these on sale?
B. Yes. They're on sale for _____.
A. Great. I'll take them.
B. Cash, check, or charge?
A. Check.

1 $7.00

2 $12.95

3 $14.99

4 $6.99

5 $9.75

6 $1.99

7 $29.99

8 $24.95

9 $23.00

10 $64.99

11 $35.00

12 $12.99

CULTURAL VIEWFINDER

In some countries the customer pays the price on the price tag. In other countries the customer can *bargain*: the customer talks with a salesperson and they agree on a price. Compare pricing in different countries you know. In your opinion, which type of pricing is better?

TALK ABOUT IT

What stores are good places to buy clothing in your area? When do they have sales? How do people find out about the sales?

Did You Hear?

DO YOU HAVE THIS IN A MEDIUM?

Listen to the conversation. Circle the size you hear.

1	(medium)	small
2	large	medium
3	X-large	petite

4	32	34
5	10	12
6	14	40

WHAT DO YOU THINK?

Listen to the conversation. Check the picture that describes the problem.

1.  ✔  ___   2. 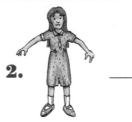 ___  ___

3. ___  ___   4. ___  ___

5. ___  ___   6.  ___  ___

IT'S ON SALE FOR $15.00

Listen to the conversation. Circle the sale price you hear.

1	($15.00)	$50.00
2	$23.00	$2.00
3	$11.79	$1.79

4	$2.99	$12.95
5	$65.99	$56.99
6	$30.99	$13.99

Check the Tag!

Clothing tags have lots of information. Can you read these tags?
Underline the size. Circle the price.

1

107883
H4001
WHITE

— SIZE —

36

$**24.00**

2

30 DEPT.	27 CLASS	05 SUB

277665-700066

SKU

449

SIZE L

OUR PRICE

$**8.99**

3

916 834 82

MDSE NO.

152	65	M31
DEPT.	CL	SEA

401	24074
VENDOR	STYLE

14 Q 8052

M

4

BUY
2 &
SAVE

2
for
$**15**

size   12

5

221757-00-1
0001

SMALL

$30.00

6

Supp. 15161-3

Size
2T

D325 9041

>$23.00

7

22.00

061 2	107883
DPT/CL	H4017

502	64	6X
SEASON	CLR	SIZE

DPT / CL / RETAIL

8

REGULAR FIT

GIRLS

100% COTTON

BARELY BLUE
530-2537

SIZE
6   S
152   P

$21.99

115

LifeWriter

WRITING CHECKS

You can pay for things at a store in different ways. You can use cash, a credit card, or a check. On a check you need to write the amount in numbers and in words.

1	one	11	eleven	21	twenty-one
2	two	12	twelve	30	thirty
3	three	13	thirteen	40	forty
4	four	14	fourteen	50	fifty
5	five	15	fifteen	60	sixty
6	six	16	sixteen	70	seventy
7	seven	17	seventeen	80	eighty
8	eight	18	eighteen	90	ninety
9	nine	19	nineteen	100	one hundred
10	ten	20	twenty	1000	one thousand

Maria Escobar bought some things at Macky's yesterday. This is her receipt and her check.

Most stores ask to see your driver's license or other picture ID when you pay by check.

MACKY'S

```
0309 40956
WOMEN'S WEAR      14.99

0309 42095
WOMEN'S WEAR      11.96

0612 5783
WOMEN'S WEAR      19.99

Subtotal          46.94
Tax 4.5%           2.11
Total             49.05
```

Thanks for shopping at Macky's

MARIA ESCOBAR
50 Booth St.
Rego Park, NY 11374

Date   1743
February 12 19 *99*

Name of Store   Amount in numbers

Pay to the
order of   *Macky's* $ *49.05*

Forty – nine and 05/100
                                            Dollars
Amount in words

For   *Maria Escobar*
                        Signature

057009345 2000423534 1743

Here are some store receipts. Can you write the checks to pay for the clothing?

```
        W E  R  K I D S
GLOVES
6924 00027          12.50
HAT
1657 70031           5.00
DENIM DRESS
2214 90887          30.00

SUBTOTAL            47.50
4.500% TAX           2.14
TOTAL               49.64
```

```
                              1744
                    _____ 19 ____

Pay to the
order of _____ $ _____

_____ Dollars

For _____    _____

057009345 2000423534 1744
```

```
      H E R A L D ' S

335-920  QTY 1      17.49
LIZ SPORT
401-663  QTY 1       8.99
SM CAS WEAR
4.5% TAX             1.19

TOTAL 02/24/99      27.67
```

```
                              1745
                    _____ 19 ____

Pay to the
order of _____ $ _____

_____ Dollars

For _____    _____

057009345 2000423534 1745
```

```
       EASTROM
995 56  MEN'S WEAR   11.00
334 92  MEN'S WEAR    9.90
665 87  MEN'S WEAR   24.00
97 1 33  MEN'S WEAR  22.00
098 54  MEN'S WEAR   69.00

SUBTOTAL            135.90
SALES TAX             6.12
Eastrom 00000       142.02

TOTAL 02/24/99      142.02
```

```
                              1746
                    _____ 19 ____

Pay to the
order of _____ $ _____

_____ Dollars

For _____    _____

057009345 2000423534 1746
```

```
JOHNSON & SMITH

Leather JACKET
37325-0006         297.99

SUB                297.99
Tax 6.0%            17.88

TOTAL              315.87
```

```
                              1747
                    _____ 19 ____

Pay to the
order of _____ $ _____

_____ Dollars

For _____    _____

057009345 2000423534 1747
```

Attention, Shoppers!

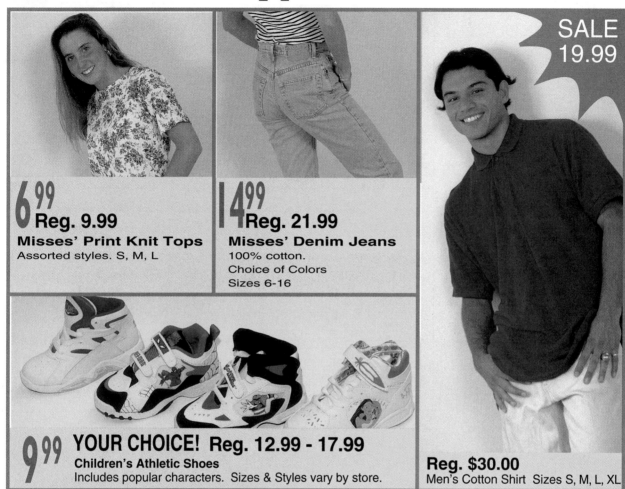

6⁹⁹ Reg. 9.99
Misses' Print Knit Tops
Assorted styles. S, M, L

14⁹⁹ Reg. 21.99
Misses' Denim Jeans
100% cotton.
Choice of Colors
Sizes 6-16

SALE
19.99

Reg. $30.00
Men's Cotton Shirt Sizes S, M, L, XL

9⁹⁹ **YOUR CHOICE!** Reg. 12.99 - 17.99
Children's Athletic Shoes
Includes popular characters. Sizes & Styles vary by store.

Newspapers are a good place to find out what's on sale. Here's an advertisement for a clothing store. Can you answer the questions?

1. How much do the jeans usually cost? _____

2. What's the sale price of the jeans? _____

3. What's another name for a blouse? _____

4. What sizes does the knit top come in? _____

5. How much is the men's shirt on sale? _____

6. What sizes does the men's shirt come in? _____

7. What are the regular prices of the shoes? _____

8. How much are the children's shoes on sale? _____

9. How much do you save on the knit top? _____

10. How much do you save on the jeans? _____

NAVIGATOR CAREER PROFILE

Sugeng Sukolono, Sales Associate

Q: What's your job?

A: I'm a sales associate in the men's department of a large department store.

Q: What exactly do you do?

A: I do many things. I arrange clothing, put up signs, and take inventory. And most important—I help customers and work at the cash register.

Q: How do you help customers?

A: I help them find what they're looking for. Sometimes they're looking for the correct size. Sometimes they're looking for a certain color.

Q: What kinds of clothing do you sell?

A: We have dress clothes and casual clothes. Sometimes a customer isn't sure if a shirt is a dress shirt or a sport shirt. I show him the difference.

Q: Do you enjoy your work?

A: Well, it's okay. I get good benefits for myself and my family. That's important.

WHAT DO YOU THINK?

What other departments are there in Sugeng's store?

What's the difference between dress clothes and casual clothes?

What benefits does Sugeng get? Why are the benefits important?

YOU'RE INVITED!

It's nice to receive an invitation! There are invitations for all different kinds of celebrations. At some celebrations people wear casual clothes, and at other celebrations they wear dress clothes. You just received these two invitations. What clothes will you wear? Make a list for each event.

You Are Invited

To _a picnic_

Date _Sat. 8/11   12:30 pm_

Place _Rockstream Park_

RSVP _291-0638– The Smiths_

Mr. and Mrs. David P. Van Duzer
request the honor
of your presence
at the marriage of their daughter
Katherine Reed Van Duzer
to
Jesse Jaya Schaffer
on
Saturday, September 25, 1999
Seven o'clock in the evening
The Plaza Hotel

Dear Navigator

Dear Navigator,

   A person at work wore a new pair of shoes to the office yesterday. They were very nice shoes. So I asked, "Where did you buy them?" He told me the name of the store. Then I asked, "How much did they cost?" But he didn't tell me the price. He just said, "They were on sale," and he walked away. I don't understand. Did I do something wrong?

Sincerely,

Curious in Costa Mesa

Dear Curious in Costa Mesa,

   Most people like to receive compliments about their clothes. They'll usually tell you where they bought something. But many people don't like to talk about money and prices. In some cultures it's okay to ask about prices, but in other cultures people don't ask these questions.

Sincerely,

Navigator

Dear Navigator,

   I'm having a problem with my teenagers. We don't agree about the clothes they wear. They want to wear dirty jeans with holes when they go to school. When I was a child, we didn't have much money. But our clothes were always clean, and they never had holes. My mother always fixed them.

   My husband and I work hard to give our children a good life. I feel ashamed when I see my children go out in their torn clothes. What should I do?

Sincerely,

Ashamed in Atlanta

Readers: What's your opinion about *Ashamed in Atlanta's* problem? Discuss this with other students. Then answer the letter.

Dear Ashamed in Atlanta,

_____

_____

_____

_____

_____

Sincerely,

_____

Now write your own
Dear Navigator letter.

Ask a question about clothing or clothing stores. Exchange letters with a classmate, and write answers to each other's letters. Then share with the class.

STAY IN SHAPE WITH THE
Sewing-on-a-Button WORKOUT

1 Button your coat.

2 Oops! Catch the button that's falling off.

3 Take off your coat.

4 Get the sewing box.

5 Open the box.

6

7 Take out some thread.

8

Put the thread through the eye of the needle.

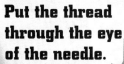

Take out a needle.

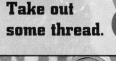

9 Tie a knot in the end.

10 Place the button on the coat.

11 Sew on the button.

12 Cut the thread.

13 Put the needle back in the sewing box.

14 Close the box.

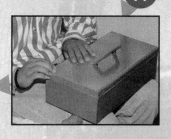

15 Put on your coat.

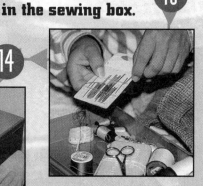

16 Button it up.

CONTRASTS
Dressed for School

Look at the photos. What are you thinking? What are you feeling?
What differences do you see?
Do you see any problems? What are the solutions?
Reflect on your own, discuss in pairs or in small groups, and share as a class.

SYNTHESIZER

Answer these questions.

Where do you shop for clothes? (Name the store.) _____

Do you usually buy clothing only when it's on sale? ☐ Yes ☐ No

How do you usually pay? ☐ cash ☐ check ☐ charge

In small groups, talk about your answers to these questions. Fill in the chart for your group. Write the number of students on each line.

HOW MANY STUDENTS	Your Group	Another Group	Another Group	Another Group	Another Group	Class Total
shop at						
shop at						
shop at						
shop at						
buy clothing only when it's on sale						
pay by cash						
pay by check						
pay by charge						

Now share as a class. Report your group's results. Fill in the other groups' results on the chart. Add up the numbers of students. Then *analyze* the information about your class. Where do students shop for clothes? How do they pay? Discuss with other students.

WordChecker

blouse
boots
coat
dress
gloves
hat
jeans
pajamas
pants
shirt
shoes
skirt
sneakers
socks
sweater
tie

big
large

long
loose
medium
short
size
small
tight

black
blue
brown
gray
green
purple
red
white
yellow

SkillChecker

I can . . .
☐ shop for clothing
☐ ask about color
☐ ask about size
☐ ask about price
☐ talk about fit
☐ read price tags
☐ read store sale ads
☐ write checks

JOURNAL

Write about a special occasion in your family— a wedding, a birthday party, or something else.

What was the occasion?
Who was there?
What did people wear?

PUZZLER PAGE

What's the object?

DESCRAMBLER

Unscramble these words about shopping for clothes. Then use the circled letters to make a new word and finish the sentence.

1. e o s l o   ① l o o s e
2. r a g l e   _ Ⓞ _ _ _
3. d u m m i e   _ _ _ _ _ Ⓞ
4. t h r o s   Ⓞ _ _ _ _
5. n o g l   Ⓞ _ _ _

I'm looking for a

_ _ _ _ _ .

Crossword

Across
2. You wear ____ when you go to bed.
5. You wear a ____ on your head.
7. You wear a ____ when it's cold.
8. You should wear a jacket and ____ at your job interview.
9. Do you have this coat in a ____ 38?

Down
1. You wear ____ on your legs.
3. You wear ____ on your feet.
4. Does this ____ look good with these pants?
6. Students like to wear blue ____ at school.

WORDRAP™

How Does It Fit?

A. How does the coat fit?
   Is it too loose or too tight?

B. It fits fine.
   But I think that the color's too bright.

A. Can I show you the same coat
   In black, brown, or gray?

B. I'm afraid I don't have time.
   Maybe some other day.

Now write your own raps about other clothing.

EZ 4 U?

Can you read the license plate?

OREGON
LV 2 SHP

⑨ The Environment

C O N V E R S A T I O N S

126 What's the Weather Forecast?

127 What Do You Want to Do Tomorrow?

128 What Are You Doing with Those Newspapers?

PREVIEW

Look at these three pictures.

Who do you think these people are?

What's happening?

What are they saying to each other?

SKILLS CHECK

Can you . . .
- [ ] *talk about the weather?*
- [ ] *get weather information?*
- [ ] *read a weather map?*
- [ ] *suggest things to do?*
- [ ] *describe locations?*
- [ ] *locate recycling centers in your area?*
- [ ] *conserve resources?*
- [ ] *follow recorded instructions on the telephone?*

What's the Weather Forecast?

A. What's the weather forecast?
B. It's going to be sunny.

Practice with a partner. Talk about weather forecasts.

A. What's the weather forecast?
B. It's going to be _____.

❶ cloudy

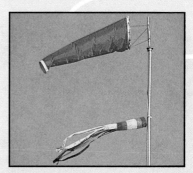

❷ windy

❸ hot

❹ cold

❺ foggy

A. What's the weather forecast?
B. It's going to _____.

❻ rain

❼ snow

What Do You Want to Do Tomorrow?

A. What do you want to do tomorrow?
B. I don't know. What's the weather going to be like?
A. According to the radio, it's going to be hot.
B. Let's go to the beach.

Practice with a partner. Decide what to do tomorrow.

A. What do you want to do tomorrow?
B. I don't know. What's the weather going to be like?
A. According to the _____, it's going to _____.
B. Let's _____.

1 newspaper

2 TV weather forecast

3 Weather Channel

4 weather information number

TALK ABOUT IT

What's your favorite kind of weather? Why?
What kind of weather don't you like? Why?
How do you find out the weather forecast?

Do you like the weather where you live?
Do you like the weather better in another place? Where? Why?

What Are You Doing with Those Newspapers?

A. What are you doing with those newspapers?
B. I'm taking them to the recycling center.
A. Oh? Where is it?
B. In the supermarket parking lot.

Practice with a partner. Tell about things you recycle.

A. What are you doing with those _____?
B. I'm taking them to the recycling center.
A. Oh? Where is it?
B. _____.

❶ **cans**
in the parking lot at the mall

❷ **jars and bottles**
behind the school

❸ **telephone books**
in back of City Hall

❹ **plastic bottles**
next to the fire station

TALK ABOUT IT

Are there recycling centers in your area?
Do you use them? What do you recycle?
Does your city pick up recyclable materials?
What's your opinion about recycling?
Is it a good idea? Is it too much trouble?
Why do you think so?

NAVIGATOR asks:

How do you conserve resources?

I *fix leaky faucets right away.*

I *recycle newspapers, glass, and plastic.*

reuse bags and containers

buy things in packages made from recycled materials

turn off the water when I brush my teeth

turn on the dishwasher only when it's full

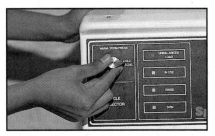
wash clothes with warm or cold water instead of hot water

take public transportation

take used car oil to the service station

take batteries to the drop-off center

ride in a carpool

Practice conversations with a partner. Talk about how you conserve resources.

A. How do you conserve resources?

B. I _____.

THINK ABOUT IT !
Why is it important to conserve resources?

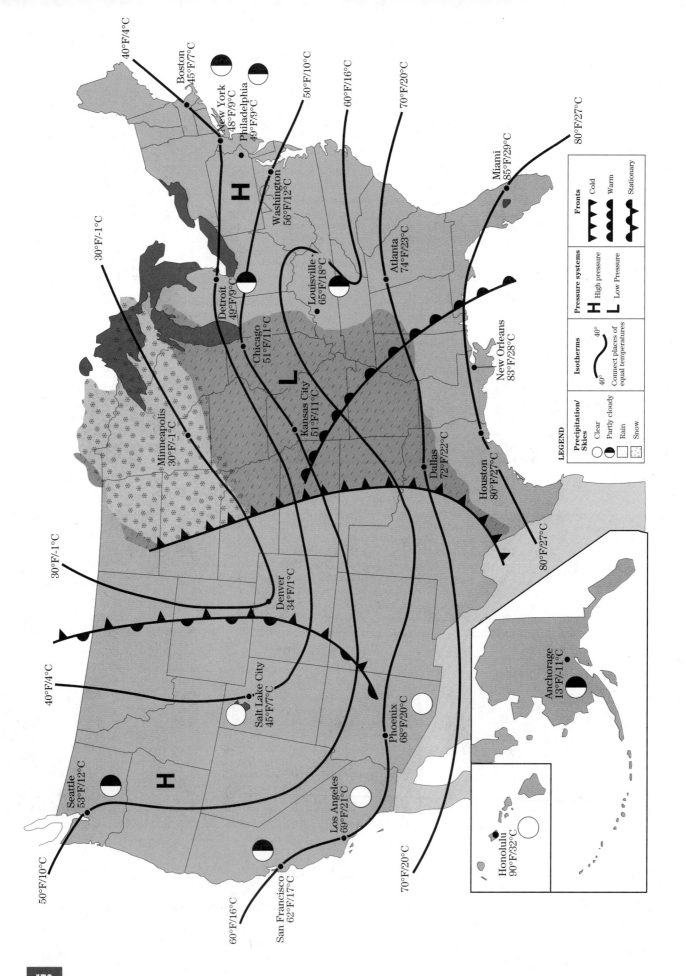

LEGEND

Precipitation/Skies
○ Clear
◑ Partly cloudy
▨ Rain
░ Snow

Isotherms
〜40° 40°
Connect places of equal temperatures

Pressure systems
H High pressure
L Low Pressure

Fronts
▼▼▼ Cold
●●● Warm
▼●▼● Stationary

40°F/4°C
Boston 45°F/7°C
New York 48°F/9°C
Philadelphia 49°F/9°C
50°F/10°C
60°F/16°C
70°F/20°C
80°F/27°C
Miami 85°F/29°C
Washington 56°F/12°C
30°F/-1°C
Detroit 49°F/9°C
Louisville 65°F/18°C
Atlanta 74°F/23°C
Chicago 51°F/11°C
New Orleans 83°F/28°C
30°F/-1°C
Minneapolis 30°F/-1°C
Kansas City 51°F/11°C
Dallas 72°F/22°C
Houston 80°F/27°C
80°F/27°C
40°F/4°C
Denver 34°F/1°C
Salt Lake City 45°F/7°C
Phoenix 68°F/20°C
Los Angeles 69°F/21°C
Anchorage 13°F/-11°C
50°F/10°C
Seattle 53°F/12°C
60°F/16°C
San Francisco 62°F/17°C
70°F/20°C
Honolulu 90°F/32°C

ALL ABOUT THE WEATHER
Check the Map!

The map on page 130 shows the **weather forecast** for many places in the United States, Canada, and Mexico. The bands of color show places with about the same temperature. The numbers under the city names show the high temperatures in degrees Fahrenheit and Celsius. Symbols on the map also give information about **precipitation** (rain or snow) and the **skies** (cloudy or clear).

Use the weather map to answer these questions. Give temperatures in both Fahrenheit and Celsius.

1. What will the high temperature be tomorrow in Los Angeles? _____

2. What will the high temperature be in Miami? _____

3. Will it be warmer tomorrow in Chicago or Vancouver? _____

4. Will there be precipitation in New York? _____

5. Where is it going to rain tomorrow? _____

6. What city on the map will have the highest temperature tomorrow? _____

THE BEST FORECAST

Compare three different weather forecasts for your area for tomorrow—in a newspaper, on the radio, and on TV. Write the information on the chart. Tomorrow evening, check the weather report on radio or TV. Write on the chart the actual weather information for that day. Which forecast was the most accurate? Share your results with your classmates. Vote for the most accurate weather forecast in your area.

	Newspaper	Radio	TV	Actual
High Temperature				
Low Temperature				
Precipitation				

**Zuni rain dance
Albuquerque, New Mexico**

CULTURAL VIEWFINDER
Different cultures believe different things about weather. For example, in some cultures people think rain on a wedding day or other special day brings good luck. What does your culture believe about weather? Share the beliefs with other students.

Did You Hear?

HERE'S TODAY'S WEATHER FORECAST

Listen to the radio weather report. Check the picture for the weather you hear.

 1  ✓ 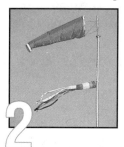 2  ___

 3 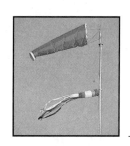 ___  4  ___

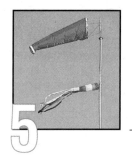 5  ___  6  ___

PRESS ONE!

Many communities have special telephone numbers you can call for information about recycling and the environment. These numbers often connect you to an automatic telephone information system. You don't talk to a person. You press telephone buttons and listen to information. Listen to this phone system. Write the correct number to press for the following information.

____ Battery drop-off centers   ____ Oil recycling

_1_ General information   ____ Ride sharing

____ Telephone book recycling   ____ Recycling program

____ Leaf collection

Sarah Thang, Extension Agent

Q: What is an extension agent?

A: Extension agents work for local cooperative extension agencies. We are part of the U.S. Department of Agriculture. We give people information about things like gardening, nutrition, and recycling.

Q: What do you do in your job?

A: I work with the recycling program. I tell people how recycling helps to protect the environment. Garbage is a big problem in this country.

Q: What can people do to help?

A: They can reduce, reuse, and recycle.

Q: What does that mean?

A: *Reduce* means make less trash. For example, when you go to the supermarket, buy food in bulk—in large containers, not in lots of little packages. *Reuse* means use something more than once. For example, you can keep plastic and paper bags to use on your next shopping trip. *Recycle* means put cans, bottles, plastic, and newspaper in recycling bins, not in the garbage.

Q: How can people find out more about recycling?

A: They can call the cooperative extension service in their area. The number is in the phone book.

WHAT DO YOU THINK?

Why is garbage a big problem?
How does recycling help to solve this problem?
What can you recycle?
What kinds of things can you buy in bulk? Why is it a good idea to do this?
What are other ways to *reduce* and *reuse*? List as many ways as you can.

SARAH THANG'S BRAINSTORMING EXERCISE

When Sarah Thang talks to people about recycling, she asks them to brainstorm ways they can reduce, reuse, and recycle. Here's one problem she gives them. Work in pairs or small groups and answer the problem. Make a list of all your ideas. Then share your ideas with the class.

You buy a large jar of peanut butter at the supermarket. You make 75 sandwiches. Now the jar is empty. How many ways can you reuse this jar?

CULTURAL VIEWFINDER

Compare recycling in different countries you know. Do people there reduce, reuse, and recycle? Do people try to protect the environment?

Dear Navigator

Dear Navigator,

Yesterday I changed the oil in my car. I was very careful. I didn't spill any oil on the street. I poured it down the sewer. My neighbor saw this and got upset. She said this is illegal. She talked about fish in the ocean, but I didn't understand her very well. The ocean is far from here.

Sincerely,

Oil Change in Orlando

Dear Oil Change in Orlando,

You spilled the oil into a storm drain. This collects rain water from the street and returns it to streams, rivers, and oceans. The oil pollutes this water, and it hurts birds, fish, and other wildlife. You can recycle your oil. Ask at the store where you buy it. Or call your local recycling program for information.

Sincerely,

Navigator

Dear Navigator,

I come from a country where it is hot and sunny most of the year. The rainy season is a very short time, and it rains only in the afternoon. Now I'm living in the Northwest, and I'm miserable. In the winter it's cold and dark. Most days are cloudy and rainy. I don't see the sun very often. I feel sad and tired all the time. I don't want to get up. I don't want to do anything. Is something wrong with me? What can I do?

Sincerely,

Pale in Portland

Readers: What's your opinion about *Pale in Portland's* problem? Discuss this with other students. Then answer the letter.

Dear Pale in Portland,

_____

_____

_____

_____

Sincerely,

_____

Now write your own
Dear Navigator letter.

Ask a question about the environment or the weather. Exchange letters with a classmate, and write answers to each other's letters. Then share with the class.

STAY IN SHAPE WITH THE
Recycling Center WORKOUT

1 Load the car.

2 Drive to the recycling center.

3 Unload the car.

4 Put the newspapers in the newspaper bin.

5 Put the clear glass in the clear glass bin.

6 Put the green glass in the green glass bin.

7 Put the brown glass in the brown glass bin.

8 Put the cans in the aluminum bin.

9 Put the plastic containers in the plastic bin.

10 Put the batteries in the battery drop-off container.

11 Drive home.

CONTRASTS
Our Water

- Look at the photos. What are you thinking? What are you feeling?
- What differences do you see?
- Do you see any problems? What are the solutions?
- Reflect on your own, discuss in pairs or in small groups, and share as a class.

SYNTHESIZER

Check the sentences that are true for you.

COOPERATIVE TEAM · INFORMATION SKILLS

Acquiring
Organizing
Communicating
Analyzing

- ☐ I buy things in bulk.
- ☐ I reuse bags and other things.
- ☐ I recycle newspapers.
- ☐ I recycle glass.
- ☐ I recycle plastic.
- ☐ I recycle cans.
- ☐ I recycle batteries.

In small groups, talk about students' answers. Fill in the chart for your group. Write the number of students on each line.

HOW MANY STUDENTS	Your Group	Another Group	Another Group	Another Group	Another Group	Class Total
buy things in bulk?						
reuse bags and other things?						
recycle newspapers?						
recycle glass?						
recycle plastic?						
recycle cans?						
recycle batteries?						

Now share as a class. Report your group's results. Fill in the other groups' results on the chart. Add up the numbers of students. Then *analyze* the information. How many students reduce, reuse, and recycle? Then discuss why and how.

WordChecker

cloudy
foggy
rain
snow
sunny
windy
cold
hot

drop-off center
environment

recycle
recycling center
reduce
reuse

bottle
can
jar
newspaper
plastic

SkillChecker

I can . . .
- ☐ talk about the weather
- ☐ get weather information
- ☐ read a weather map
- ☐ suggest things to do
- ☐ describe locations
- ☐ locate recycling centers in my area
- ☐ conserve resources
- ☐ follow recorded instructions on the telephone

JOURNAL

Write about a day in your life when the weather was terrible or beautiful.

What was the weather like?
What happened?
How did you feel?
Why do you remember that day?

PUZZLER PAGE

CLOSE-UP

What's the object?

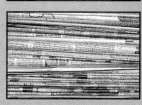

WordSearcher

Can you find the words?

```
Z W S U N G V O M W
W Q E N H G Z Z B U
I L X A O I L N N T
N O Z C T W X X V P
D T W B O H I W Y O
W K J O K L E F A B
B L C L O U D R P K
O I Q G R A I N O L
Q P G O N B E L X Z
Z X O G G Q K I K H
```

COLD	WEATHER	HOT
SNOW	RAIN	CLOUD
SUN	WIND	

EZ 4 U?

Can you read these license plates?

DESCRAMBLER

Unscramble these words. Then use the circled letters to make a new word and finish the sentence.

1. t r y e t a b   _b_ _a_ _t_ (_t_) _e_ (_r_) _y_
2. l o i   (○) _ _
3. s n a c   (○) _ _ _
4. c l i a s p t   (○) _ _ _ (○) _ _
5. e s r p p n a w e   _ _ _ _ _ _ _ _ (○) _

We need to _ _ _ _ _ _ _ _ **the environment.**

WORDRAP™

It Always Rains on the Weekend

*It always rains on the
  weekend.
It's always cold and dark.
It's always cloudy on the
  weekend
When we're planning a picnic
  in the park.*

*It's always sunny on weekdays
When we have to go to work
  or school.
It's never nice on the weekend
When we want to swim at a
  beach or a pool.*

10 Your Family

CONVERSATIONS

140 What's Your Son's Last Name?

141 Can You Please Sign This Permission Slip?

142 Please Help Me! My Daughter is Lost!

PREVIEW

Look at these three pictures.

Who do you think these people are?

What's happening?

What are they saying to each other?

SKILLS CHECK

Can you . . .

☐ *register a child for school?*
☐ *fill out a registration form?*
☐ *understand and fill out a permission slip?*
☐ *report a missing child?*
☐ *describe people?*

What's Your Son's Last Name?

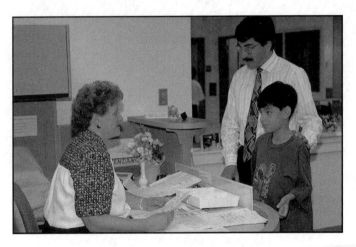

A. May I help you?

B. Yes, please. I'm here to register my son for school.

A. Okay. What's your son's last name?

B. Hassan.

A. And his first name?

B. Abdi.

A. How old is he?

B. Six.

Practice with a partner. Register a child for school.

A. May I help you?

B. Yes, please. I'm here to register my _____ for school.

A. Okay. What's your _____'s last name?

B. _____.

A. And _____ first name?

B. _____.

A. How old is _____?

B. _____.

1 **daughter**
Jennifer Crowley
5

2 **niece**
Glenda Wilson
10

3 **nephew**
Lamont Adams
5

CULTURAL VIEWFINDER

At what age do children start school in different countries you know? How many years do children go to school in different countries? How many days a week? How many hours a day?

Can You Please Sign This Permission Slip?

A. Can you please sign this permission slip?
B. What's it for?
A. Our class is going on a field trip.
B. Where are you going?
A. To the museum.
B. Okay.

Practice with a partner. Tell where you are going.

A. Can you please sign this permission slip?
B. What's it for?
A. Our class is going on a field trip.
B. Where are you going?
A. To the _____.
B. Okay.

fire station

art gallery

planetarium

concert hall

nature center

zoo

A parent must sign a permission slip before a child can go on a field trip.

Please Help Me! My Daughter is Lost!

A. **Please help me! My daughter is lost!**
B. **How old is she?**
A. **Five.**
B. **What does she look like?**
A. **She's short, and she has long brown hair.**
B. **What's she wearing?**
A. **Blue pants and a purple jacket.**
B. **Okay. Wait here. Don't worry. We'll find her.**

Practice with a partner. The people on page 143 are missing. Describe them.

A. Please help me! My _____ is lost!
B. How old is _____?
A. _____.
B. What does _____ look like?
A. _____.
B. What's _____ wearing?
A. _____.
B. Okay. Wait here. Don't worry. We'll find _____.

WAYS TO DESCRIBE PEOPLE

tall

short

heavy

thin

long hair

short hair

straight hair

curly hair

bald

1 son

2 sister

3 brother

4 mother

5 nephew

6 father

DO YOU HAVE A PHOTOGRAPHIC MEMORY?

Look carefully at everybody in your classroom. Notice their clothing. Think about what they look like. Then leave the room with another student. Describe a classmate. Can your partner give the student's name? Return to class. Was your description correct?

TIPS FOR CHILD SAFETY

Can young children in your family say their first and last names? Can they say *your* name? Do they know their address and telephone number? Do they know what to do if they get lost? Do they know that they should never go anywhere with a stranger? Talk with them about safety.

Many cities have child I.D. programs. The police take a child's photograph and fingerprints and they give you an I.D. card. Ask about the child I.D. program in your area.

Did You Hear?

WHAT'S YOUR SON'S FIRST NAME?

Listen to the question. Circle the correct answer.

1	7	(John)	5	17	613
2	10	Mary	6	Clinton	heavy
3	jeans	tall	7	sweater	straight
4	curly	a T-shirt	8	short	shirt

WHAT DOES HE LOOK LIKE?

Listen to the description. Check the correct picture.

1 ✓

2

3

4

LifeWriter

SCHOOL REGISTRATION FORM

When you register a child for school you need to fill out many forms. Fill out this registration form for your child or a child you know.

REQUEST FOR ENTRANCE

Child's Name _____ Date _____
             Last   First   Middle

Address

_____
Number   Street   Apt #   Zip Code

Telephone _____ ☐ male   ☐ female

Place of Birth _____ Date of Birth _____

Father's Name   Mother's Name

_____   _____
Last   First   Middle Initial   Last   First   Middle Initial

Occupation   Occupation

_____   _____

Work Telephone   Work Telephone

_____   _____

Name of friend or relative to contact in case of emergency:

_____ _____ _____
Name   Address   Telephone

Names of brothers and sisters

	Last	First	Middle			Birthdate
1.				M	F	
2.				M	F	
3.				M	F	
4.				M	F	
5.				M	F	

LifeWriter

Children bring many papers home from school. Some papers are permission slips. You need to sign a permission slip and return it to the teacher. Fill in these permission slips and sign them. Then answer the questions.

FIELD TRIP NOTE OF PERMISSION

Destination _Fire Station_____ Date _May 29____ Time ____10:00___

School Bus   Chartered Bus   Private Automobile   (Walking)

Purpose _Learn about fire safety_____   Expense _____

_Mr. Ross_____
(Teacher)

Name of Pupil _____

This pupil has my permission to go on the field trip as indicated above.

_____
(Parent or Guardian)

1

Where are the students going?
How much will it cost?
When are they going?
How will they get there?
Why are they going?

FIELD TRIP NOTE OF PERMISSION

Destination _Concert Hall_____ Date _October 12___ Time ____9:30___

(School Bus)   Chartered Bus   Private Automobile   Walking

Purpose _Young People's Concert—Learn About Orchestra_ Expense _$2.50___

_Mrs. Copes_____
(Teacher)

Name of Pupil _____

This pupil has my permission to go on the field trip as indicated above.

_____
(Parent or Guardian)

2

Where are the students going?
How much will it cost?
When are they going?
How will they get there?
Why are they going?

NAVIGATOR CAREER PROFILE

Marta Santiago, Child-Care Provider

Q: How many children do you watch?

A: Right now I have four children in my home. One is just an infant. The others are 18 months, 2, and 3.

Q: How many hours are these children with you?

A: Their parents usually drop them off around 8:00. They pick them up by 6:00.

Q: What do you do all day?

A: I have many activities for my children. I have many different toys. I read books. They color and paint. Every day we take a walk or play in the park. They take a nap in the afternoon.

Q: What about food?

A: I give them a healthy snack in the morning, lunch at 12:30, and another healthy snack in the afternoon.

WHAT DO YOU THINK?

Why do these children need a child-care provider? What did Marta study in her child-care class? What kind of snacks does she give the children? In your opinion, is this a good place for these children? Why or why not?

Q: Is it a difficult job?

A: It can be. I don't take care of too many children at one time. There are laws about that. I took a class about child care at the adult education center. I learned a lot about how to take care of children. I'm very careful. Some toys have small pieces. I don't buy those toys. Some foods are dangerous, too. I don't feed my children nuts, popcorn, or grapes.

Q: You call them "your children."

A: Oh, yes. I love these children very much, just like they're my own. I know it's hard for parents to leave their little ones with a baby-sitter all day. I try to give the children the love and attention a parent gives.

ADS   ADS   ADS

Child-care providers often advertise in the newspaper and on community bulletin boards. Parents who are looking for baby-sitters also advertise. Look on bulletin boards. Read the classified ads in your newspaper. Write down ads about child care, bring them to class, and discuss them with other students.

Dear Navigator

Dear Navigator,

    Today I saw something very strange at the mall. A mother was walking with her child. The mother was holding one end of a long rope. The other end was attached to the little girl's wrist. The girl looked sad. I think leashes are for dogs and not for children. What do you think?

          Sincerely,

Mall Shopper in Milwaukee

Dear Mall Shopper in Milwaukee,

    Shopping malls are large and crowded. It is easy for a small child to get lost. There are also many escalators. These can be dangerous for a young child. Some parents use these things to keep their children safe. It looks strange, but it's really for the child's safety.

          Sincerely,

Navigator

Dear Navigator,

    I have a two-year-old son. I want to stay home with him, but we need money. I have to go back to work. I see stories on TV about bad baby-sitters. I am very worried. How can I find a good, safe baby-sitter for my son? My parents are back in my country, so that isn't the answer. I'm afraid something terrible is going to happen. What can I do?

          Sincerely,

Anxious Parent in Anaheim

Readers: What's your opinion about *Anxious Parent in Anaheim's* problem? Discuss this with other students. Then answer the letter.

Dear Anxious Parent in Anaheim,

_____

_____

_____

          Sincerely,

      _____

Now write your own
Dear Navigator letter.

Ask a question or give an opinion about parenting. Exchange letters with a classmate, and write answers to each other's letters. Then share with the class.

Playground WORKOUT

1 Take the kids to the playground.

2 Swing on the swings.

3 Crawl through the tunnel.

5 Slide down the slide.

4 Climb up the ladder.

6 Go across the monkey bars.

7 Play in the sandbox.

8 Spin around.

10 Rest!

9 Go up and down on the seesaw.

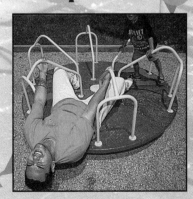

CONTRASTS
A Place to Play

- Look at the photos. What are you thinking? What are you feeling?
- What are the situations? What differences do you see?
- Do you see any problems? What are the solutions?
- Reflect on your own, discuss in pairs or in small groups, and share as a class.

SYNTHESIZER

Acquiring
Organizing
Communicating
Analyzing

Check the sentences that are true for you.

I can give information on
a form about:

☐ my personal information
☐ my family members
☐ my work experience
☐ my medical history

When I fill out a
difficult form:

☐ I don't ask for help.
☐ I ask a family member for help.
☐ I ask a friend or neighbor for help.
☐ I ask somebody at that office for help.

In small groups, talk about students' answers to these questions. Fill in the chart for your group. Write the number of students on each line.

HOW MANY STUDENTS		Your Group	Another Group	Another Group	Another Group	Another Group	Class Total
can give information about	themselves?						
	family members?						
	work experience?						
	medical history?						
don't ask for help?							
ask a family member for help?							
ask a friend or neighbor for help?							
ask somebody at the office for help?							

Now share as a class. Report your group's results. Fill in the other groups' results on the chart. Add up the numbers of students. Then analyze the information. What kinds of information can students give on a form? What do students do when a form is difficult?

WordChecker

child-care
  provider
field trip
nephew
niece
permission
  slip
register
registration
  form

tall
short
heavy
thin
long hair
short hair
curly
straight
bald

SkillChecker

I can . . .

☐ register a child for school
☐ fill out a registration form
☐ understand and fill out a permission slip
☐ report a missing child
☐ describe people

JOURNAL

Write about a field trip you want to take with your class.

*Where do you want to go?
How will you get there?
What will you do there?*

PUZZLER PAGE

WordSearcher
Can you find the words?

```
T H E A T E R Z U M
I R M T A P R H U U
V M I C Z E M L D S
N G D P O B X R P E
A K L Z O N E F O U
T C X R G B C I D M
U G E C O G I E N M
R R E U L W I L R H
E Y V B O O S D P T
W (C E N T E R) Z C T
```

CENTER	MUSEUM	TRIP
FIELD	NATURE	ZOO
THEATER	CONCERT	

CLOSE-UP

What's the object?

EZ 4 U?
Can you read these license plates?

OHIO

C SAW

ONTARIO

GO 2 SKL

DESCRAMBLER
Unscramble these words. Then use the circled letters to make a new word and finish the sentence.

1. y l r u c   c u r (l) y
2. t t h i a g r s   (○) _ _ _ _ _ _
3. g o n l   _ (○) _ _
4. h i t n   (○) _ _ _
5. r o s h t   _ _ _ (○) _
6. y h a v e   _ (○)(○) _ _

I can't find my children.

They _ _ _ _ _ _ _ _ .

WORDRAP™

First Name! Last Name! Middle Initial!

First name! Last name! Middle initial!
First name! Last name! Middle initial!
Fill out the form.
Give your date of birth.
Street number, apartment number.
Don't forget your zip code.
Home phone, work phone.
Write down your area code.
Check male or female.
List the people in your family.
Give your occupation.
Please write legibly.
First name! Last name! Middle initial!
First name! Last name! Middle initial!

Page 9 **WHAT'S YOUR TELEPHONE NUMBER?**

Listen and circle the numbers you hear.

1. A. What's your telephone number?
   B. Four-six-two-eight-nine-three-four.
   A. Four-six-two-eight-nine-three-four?
   B. Yes, that's right.

2. A. What's your phone number?
   B. Seven-eight-six-two-one-six-five.
   A. Seven-eight-six-two-one-six-five?
   B. Yes, that's right.

3. A. And your telephone number?
   B. It's two-three-seven-one-two-three-four.
   A. Two-three-seven-one-two-three-four?
   B. Uh-húh.

4. A. What's your apartment number?
   B. It's two-fifteen.
   A. Two-fifteen?
   B. Uh-húh.

5. A. Your apartment number please?
   B. Five twenty-four.
   A. Five twenty-four?
   B. Yes, that's right.

6. A. What's your address?
   B. Eleven thirty-five Nelson Street.
   A. Eleven thirty-five?
   B. Yes, that's right.

7. A. And your address?
   B. Forty-two oh nine Glen Avenue.
   A. Forty-two oh nine?
   B. Yes.

8. A. Your address please?
   B. Thirteen thirteen Maple Court.
   A. Thirteen thirteen?
   B. Yes, that's right.

Page 9 **COULD YOU SPELL THAT PLEASE?**

Listen and fill in the missing letters.

1. A. What's your last name?
   B. Smith.
   A. Could you spell that please?
   B. S-M-I-T-H.
   A. S-M-I-T-H. Thank you.

2. A. What's your first name?
   B. Carlos.
   A. Could you spell that please?
   B. C-A-R-L-O-S.
   A. C-A-R-L-O-S. Thank you.

3. A. What's your first name?
   B. Tuan.

A. Please spell that.
   B. T-U-A-N.
   A. T-U-A-N. Thank you.

4. A. What's your name?
   B. Abdul.
   A. Spell that, please.
   B. A-B-D-U-L.
   A. A-B-D-U-L.

5. A. And your last name?
   B. Peters.
   A. Spell that, please.
   B. P-E-T-E-R-S.
   A. P-E-T-E-R-S.

6. A. And your first name?
   B. Tony.
   A. T-O-N-Y?
   B. Yes, that's right.

7. A. What's your first name?
   B. Allen.
   A. How do you spell that?
   B. A-L-L-E-N.
   A. A-L-L-E-N?
   B. Yes.

8. A. And your last name?
   B. Collins.
   A. How do you spell that?
   B. C-O-L-L-I-N-S.
   A. C-O-L-L-I-N-S?
   B. Yes, that's right.

Page 9 **WHAT'S YOUR LAST NAME?**

Listen to the question and circle the correct answer.

1. A. What's your last name?
   B. Excuse me?
   A. What's your last name?

2. A. What's your last name?
   B. Excuse me?
   A. What's your last name?

3. A. What's your telephone number?
   B. Excuse me?
   A. Your phone number?

4. A. What's your apartment number?
   B. Excuse me?
   A. What's your apartment number?

5. A. What's your address?
   B. Excuse me?
   A. What's your address?

6. A. What's your phone number?
   B. Pardon me?
   A. What's your phone number?

7. A. Your phone number, please.
   B. Pardon me?
   A. Your phone number?

8. A. And your social security number?
   B. What was that?
   A. Your social security number?

Page 22 **WHAT'S THE WARNING SIGN?**

Listen to the warnings and check the correct sign.

1. A. Careful! Don't go in there!
   B. Excuse me?
   A. The sign says *Do Not Enter*.
   B. Oh. Thanks.

2. A. Be careful! You need to wear your safety glasses.
   B. Excuse me?
   A. The sign says *Safety Glasses Required*.
   B. Oh. Thanks.

3. A. Watch it! Don't go out that way!
   B. Excuse me?
   A. The sign says *Emergency Exit Only*.
   B. Oh. Thanks.

4. A. Careful! Don't walk there!
   B. Excuse me?
   A. The sign says *Caution Wet Floor!*
   B. Oh. Thanks.

5. A. Look out! Don't sit there!
   B. Excuse me?
   A. The sign says *Wet Paint*.
   B. Oh. Thanks.

6. A. Be careful! Put on your helmet.
   B. Excuse me?
   A. The sign says *Helmets Required*.
   B. Oh. Thanks.

Page 22 **WHAT'S YOUR WORK SCHEDULE?**

Listen to the conversations about schedules. Circle the day you hear.

1. A. Can I have Monday off?
   B. Monday? Sure. No problem.

2. A. Can I have Friday off?
   B. Friday? Sure. No problem.

3. A. Can you work Saturday?
   B. Saturday? Sure. No problem.

4. A. Can I have Wednesday off?
   B. Wednesday? Sure. No problem.

5. A. Can you work Sunday?
   B. Sunday? Sure. No problem.

6. A. Can you work Tuesday?
   B. Tuesday? Sure. No problem.

THAT'LL BE $4.89

Listen to the cashier. Circle the amount you hear.

1. A. That'll be four dollars and eighty-nine cents.
   B. Four eighty-nine. Here you are.

2. A. That'll be five dollars and thirty-two cents.
   B. Five thirty-two. Here you are.

3. A. That'll be two dollars and ninety-eight cents.
   B. Two ninety-eight. Here you are.

4. A. That'll be eight dollars and forty-seven cents.
   B. Eight forty-seven. Here you are.

5. A. That'll be seventy-six dollars and thirty-four cents.
   B. Seventy-six thirty-four. Here you are.

6. A. That'll be twenty-four dollars and forty-seven cents.
   B. Twenty-four forty-seven. Here you are.

7. A. That'll be sixteen dollars and seventy-three cents.
   B. Sixteen seventy-three. Here you are.

8. A. That'll be forty dollars and ninety-two cents.
   B. Forty ninety-two. Here you are.

ARE YOU READY TO ORDER?

Listen to the customers and put a check next to each item ordered.

1. A. Are you ready to order?
   B. Yes. I'll have a hamburger and a medium Coke.
   A. That's a hamburger and a medium Coke, right?
   B. Uh-húh.

2. A. Are you ready to order?
   B. Yes. I'll have a chicken sandwich and a large coffee.
   A. That's a chicken sandwich and a large coffee, right?
   B. Uh-húh.

3. A. Are you ready to order?
   B. Yes. I'll have a cheeseburger and a medium iced tea.
   A. That's a cheeseburger and a medium iced tea, right?
   B. Uh-húh.

4. A. Are you ready to order?
   B. Yes. I'll have a fish sandwich and a small milk.
   A. That's a fish sandwich and a small milk, right?
   B. Uh-húh.

EMERGENCY!

Listen and circle the correct response.

1. What's your name?
2. What's your telephone number?
3. What's your address?
4. What's your apartment number?
5. What's your address?
6. And your phone number?

WHAT'S THE SCHEDULE?

Listen to the recorded announcement. Circle the correct information.

1. The clinic is open daily from nine to five.
2. The personnel office is open daily from eight-thirty to two-thirty.
3. Immunizations are given on Wednesdays from eight to four.
4. You can apply for a marriage license in room 10A from nine to five-thirty, Monday through Friday.
5. The dental clinic is open Tuesday from nine to five.
6. Road test appointments can be made by calling 561-3429 Monday from eight to four-thirty.
7. Registration for the next session is Tuesday and Thursday from nine to twelve.
8. For general information, call Monday through Friday from nine to four.

HOW MUCH IS IT?

Listen to the conversation at the post office. Circle the amount you hear.

1. A. Anything else?
   B. No, that's all.
   A. That's seventy-two cents.
   B. Seventy-two cents. Here you are.

2. A. Anything else?
   B. A book of stamps, please.
   A. That comes to ten dollars.
   B. Ten dollars. Here you are.

3. A. That'll be eighty-five cents.
   B. Let's see. Eighty-five cents.
   A. Thank you.

4. A. That'll be two eighty-three.
   B. Let's see. Two eighty-three.
   A. Thank you.

5. A. That comes to one seventy.
   B. Here you are. One seventy.

6. A. That comes to fifty-five cents.
   B. Here you are. Fifty-five cents.

7. A. Your total is six fifteen.
   B. Six fifteen?
   A. Yes.

8. A. Your total is three seventy-three.
   B. Three seventy-three?
   A. Yes.

THERE'S SOMETHING WRONG WITH MY OVEN

Listen to the conversations about problems and check the correct picture.

1. A. This is Alice Jones in apartment fifty-five. There's something wrong with my oven.
   B. Your oven? Okay. We'll send someone over to look at it.

2. A. This is Marcos Ortega in apartment one-oh-one. There's something wrong with my heat.
   B. Your heat? Okay. We'll send someone over to check it.

3. A. This is Binh Le in apartment twenty-one-A. There's something wrong with my sink.
   B. Your sink? Okay. We'll send someone over to look at it.

4. A. This is Lisa Simpson in apartment three-twenty-six. There's something wrong with my air conditioner.
   B. Your air conditioner? Okay. We'll send someone over to look at it.

5. A. This is Fred Rogers in apartment four-fourteen. There's something wrong with my lock.
   B. Your lock? Okay. We'll send someone over to look at it.

6. A. This is Faduma Yusuf in apartment five. There's something wrong with my dishwasher.
   B. Your dishwasher? Okay. We'll send someone over to look at it.

I'D LIKE TO BUY A MONEY ORDER

Listen to the people ask for money orders and circle the amount you hear.

1. A. I'd like to buy a money order for five hundred fifty dollars.
   B. Did you say five hundred fifteen or five hundred fifty?
   A. Five hundred fifty. Five-five-oh.

2. A. I'd like to buy a money order for three hundred thirteen dollars.
   B. Did you say three hundred thirteen or three hundred thirty?
   A. Three hundred thirteen. Three-one-three.

3. A. I'd like to buy a money order for seven hundred sixty dollars.

B. Did you say seven hundred sixteen or seven hundred sixty?
A. Seven hundred sixty. Seven-six-oh.

4. A. I'd like to buy a money order for four hundred seventy dollars.
   B. Did you say four hundred seventeen or four hundred seventy?
   A. Four hundred seventy. Four-seven-oh.

5. A. I'd like to buy a money order for five hundred eighteen dollars.
   B. Did you say five hundred eighteen or five hundred eighty?
   A. Five hundred eighteen. Five-one-eight.

6. A. I'd like to buy a money order for six hundred forty dollars.
   B. Did you say six hundred fourteen or six hundred forty?
   A. Six hundred forty. Six-four-oh.

7. A. I'd like to buy a money order for two hundred ninety dollars.
   B. Did you say two hundred nineteen or two hundred ninety?
   A. Two hundred ninety. Two-nine-oh.

8. A. I'd like to buy a money order for four hundred fifteen dollars.
   B. Did you say four hundred fifteen or four hundred fifty?
   A. Four hundred fifteen. Four-one-five.

CAN YOU COME ON THURSDAY AT 3:00?

Listen to the conversations between patients and receptionists. Circle the correct appointment time.

1. A. Can you come on Thursday at three o'clock?
   B. Thursday at three? Yes, that'll be fine.

2. A. Can you come in on Wednesday at twelve fifteen?
   B. Wednesday at twelve fifteen? Yes, that'll be fine.

3. A. Can you come on Tuesday at ten thirty?
   B. Tuesday at ten thirty? Yes, that'll be fine.

4. A. Can you come in on Friday at four o'clock?
   B. Friday at four? Yes, that'll be fine.

5. A. Can you come on Thursday at two o'clock?
   B. Thursday at two? Yes, that'll be fine.

6. A. Can you come in on Tuesday at eleven fifteen?
   B. Tuesday at eleven fifteen? Yes, that'll be fine.

TAKE TWO TABLETS WITH MEALS

Listen to each conversation between a customer and a pharmacist. Check the correct label.

1. A. How much should I take?
   B. Take two tablets with meals.
   A. Two tablets with meals. All right. Thank you.

2. A. How much should I take?
   B. Take two teaspoons every four hours.
   A. Two teaspoons every four hours. All right. Thank you.

3. A. How much should I take?
   B. Take two pills every three hours.
   A. Two pills every three hours. All right. Thank you.

4. A. How much should I take?
   B. Take two capsules as needed.
   A. Two capsules as needed. All right. Thank you.

5. A. How much should I take?
   B. Take one teaspoon three times a day.
   A. One teaspoon three times a day. All right. Thank you.

6. A. How much should I take?
   B. Take one pill after meals.
   A. One pill after meals. All right. Thank you.

I'M LOOKING FOR A BANK

Listen to the conversations. Check the locations you hear.

1. A. Excuse me. I'm looking for a bank.
   B. There's a bank next to the post office.
   A. Next to the post office? Thanks.

2. A. Excuse me. I'm looking for a gas station.
   B. There's a gas station between the toy store and the supermarket.
   A. Between the toy store and the supermarket? Thanks.

3. A. Excuse me. I'm looking for a bakery.
   B. There's a bakery next to the book store.
   A. Next to the book store? Thanks.

4. A. Excuse me. I'm looking for a parking lot.

B. There's a parking lot between the bank and the hotel.
A. Between the bank and the hotel? Thanks.

5. A. Excuse me. I'm looking for a drug store.
   B. There's a drug store across from the restaurant.
   A. Across from the restaurant? Thanks.

FLIGHT 207 IS NOW BOARDING

Listen to the announcements. Circle the gate or track number you hear.

1. Flight two-oh-seven is now boarding at Gate eight. Flight two-oh-seven is now boarding at Gate eight.

2. The Continental is arriving on Track 2B. The Continental is arriving on Track 2B.

3. All aboard Track fifty-six. All aboard Track fifty-six.

4. The express bus to Miami will be leaving from Gate forty-eight. The express bus to Miami will be leaving from Gate forty-eight.

5. Flight one twenty-six is arriving at Gate seventy-three. Flight one twenty-six is arriving at Gate seventy-three.

6. Now boarding Track twenty-two. Now boarding Track twenty-two.

7. The Midnight Special is departing from Gate nineteen. The Midnight Special is departing from Gate nineteen.

8. The Orange Blossom is arriving at Track one sixty-six. The Orange Blossom is arriving at Track one sixty-six.

DO YOU HAVE THIS IN A MEDIUM?

Listen to the conversations. Circle the size you hear.

1. A. Do you have this sweater in a medium?
   B. Medium? Let me check.

2. A. Do you have this sweater in a large?
   B. Large? Let me check.

3. A. Do you have this blouse in a petite?
   B. Petite? Let me check.

4. A. Do you have this shirt in a size thirty-four?
   B. Thirty-four? Let me check.

5. A. Do you have this skirt in a size ten?
   B. Ten? Let me check.
6. A. Do you have this jacket in a size fourteen?
   B. Fourteen? Let me check.

Page 114 **WHAT DO YOU THINK?**

Listen to the conversation. Check the picture that describes the problem.

1. A. What do you think?
   B. It looks too big.
2. A. What do you think?
   B. It looks too short.
3. A. How does it fit?
   B. It's too long.
4. A. How does it fit?
   B. It's too small.
5. A. How does it fit?
   B. It's too tight.
6. A. What do you think?
   B. They're too large.

Page 114 **IT'S ON SALE FOR $15.00**

Listen to the conversation. Circle the sale price you hear.

1. A. Is this on sale?
   B. Yes. It's on sale for fifteen dollars.
2. A. Is this on sale?
   B. Yes. It's on sale for twenty-three dollars.
3. A. Is this on sale?
   B. Yes. It's on sale for one seventy-nine.
4. A. Are these on sale?
   B. Yes. They're on sale for twelve ninety-five.
5. A. Are these on sale?
   B. Yes. They're on sale for sixty-five ninety-nine.
6. A. Is this on sale?
   B. Yes. It's on sale for thirteen ninety-nine.

Page 132 **HERE'S TODAY'S WEATHER FORECAST**

Listen to the radio weather report. Check the picture for the weather you hear.

1. And here's today's weather: Cloudy, with temperatures in the 40's.
2. And here's today's weather: Clear and windy, with temperatures in the 30's.
3. A. Here's Ryan with the weather
   B. Good morning! There's a ninety percent chance of rain.
4. Today's weather report is: Mostly sunny, highs in the eighties.
5. And here is today's weather: Sunny, hot, and humid. Temperatures near one hundred.
6. Today's weather will be cold and sunny. Highs expected in the teens.

Page 132 **FOR GENERAL INFORMATION, PRESS ONE**

Many communities have special telephone numbers to call for recycling information. Listen to the phone message. Write the correct number to push for the following information.

You have reached the department of environmental services. For general information, press one.

For information about leaf collection, press 2.

For information about composting, press 3.

For oil recycling, press 4.

For information about battery drop off, press 5.

For other information about recycling, press 6.

For the RideFinders program, press 7.

Page 144 **WHAT'S YOUR SON'S FIRST NAME?**

Listen to the question. Circle the correct answer.

1. A. What's your son's first name?
   B. Excuse me?
   A. What's your son's first name?
2. A. How old is she?
   B. Excuse me?
   A. How old is she?
3. A. What does she look like?
   B. Excuse me?
   A. What does she look like?
4. A. What's he wearing?
   B. Excuse me?
   A. What's he wearing?
5. A. How old is he?
   B. Excuse me?
   A. How old is he?
6. A. What's his last name?
   B. Excuse me?
   A. What's his last name?
7. A. What's she wearing?
   B. Excuse me?
   A. What's she wearing?
8. A. What does she look like?
   B. Excuse me?
   A. What does she look like?

Page 144 **WHAT DOES HE LOOK LIKE?**

Listen to the description. Check the correct picture.

1. A. What does he look like?
   B. He's 4 years old, short, and thin.
   A. What's he wearing?
   B. A long-sleeved shirt and blue jeans.
2. A. What does she look like?
   B. She's 12, tall, and thin. And she's wearing a yellow shirt and blue and yellow shorts.
3. A. What does he look like?
   B. My father's short and thin.
   A. What's he wearing?
   B. Dark pants and a white shirt.
4. A. What does she look like?
   B. She's medium height with short hair. And she's wearing a white skirt with a blue blouse and a blue jacket.